Songs of Ourselves

America's Interior Landscape

Mary Lawlor

Paul Heller

Blue Heron Book Works, LLC

Allentown, Pennsylvania

Cover design: Angie Zambrano

ISBN: 0996817743
ISBN-13:978-0-9968177-4-5

Library of Congress Control Number: 2015919028.

Blue Heron Book Works, LLC
Allentown, PA 18104
www.blueheronbookworks.com

To Brother Walt

CONTENTS

Foreword   vi

Introduction, Mary Lawlor   1

Susan Lee Feathers   6

Tomas Benitez   14

Peter W. Fong   18

Paul Heller   29

Victoria Franzese   36

Judith Farmer Miller   46

G.B. Miller   52

G. Bruce Boyer   56

Mary Flood   67

Jonah Matranga   79

Jim Brega   92

Tom Carter   102

Patricia Wellingham-Jones   112

Raymond M. Wong   121

Ann Sonz Matranga   131

Nancy Canyon   140

Morton J. Miller   146

Gail Reitano   161

Sherry Stratton   171

Freddi Tachman Carlip   176

Linda Marsh   185

Donna Vitucci   190

Pamela Varkony   194

Nicholas DiGiovanni   199

About the Authors   208

FOREWORD

I'm always wondering what my fellow passengers on the IRT are thinking. They're every variety of human being, reading their iPhones or Stephen King, doing last minute edits on a presentation, sipping from hot to-go cups, staring out at the graffiti on the tunnel walls, thinking....what?

Only when the train breaks down do they drop their game faces and see one another—scanning for allies, just in case—retreating when the lights come back on and the train lurches forward.

The most fun you can have in life is getting to know another human being. It's especially true because devices—cell phones, earphones—conspire to keep us apart by allowing only warped sound-bite glimpses into one another's heads. How much nuance can you fit into 156 characters or an Instagram? Do the cadres of elves cramming the wisdom of Western Civ into memes really have a clue about any of us?

Blue Heron Book Works began publishing memoirs in 2014, receiving, along with full length manuscripts, an occasional small submission. We set aside a few with a flash of insight into self, reluctant to call them rejects just because of size. Journal entries about trying times in a marriage and *now* what. A bittersweet diary of a man in a mental institution battling depression with humor. Letters from a dad to his daughter at camp. Journals of people who interact with foxes, skunks, hawks, in their backyards and write about the private pleasure of knowing another species. Epiphanies of a woman retired too soon. Bits by a man distracting the grim reaper with flattery. Diaries of travelers bent on discovering who else is out there.

A note. A beat. A couple of bars. Pretty soon it began to sound like music.

*I hear the sound of a human voice. It is a sound I love.**

Blue Heron posted in the ether for more shorts: blogs, diaries, clippings, letters arrived. A stream of consciousness by an itinerant troubadour—worried about his savings account but helpless to do anything but what he was born to do: create, outcome be damned. The daughter of a big band leader sent her father's playlist of songs his band would play when celebrities entered El Morocco. Emails from a woman to her grown son whose father had just died and now he wants to know.

As serendipity would have it, a copy of Walt Whitman's *Song of Myself* was being passed around the office when the staff and editors were deciding what to do with these small pieces. One of them had an "aha!" moment. In *Song of Myself*, Whitman takes the measure of what is in front in him and in his heart with no preamble, no camouflage of self-explanation. That is what the 24 writers in *Songs of Ourselves* are doing, telling us their story, letting us see them game face off.

*I hear the chorus…it is a grand opera…this is indeed music!**

Can anything be more breathtaking than that?

Paul Heller

*Walt Whitman, *Song of Myself*

INTRODUCTION

MARY LAWLOR

*The groups of newly-come immigrants cover the
wharf or levee...
The one-year wife is recovering and happy, a
week ago she bore her first child,
The clean-haired Yankee girl works with her sewing-
machine, or in the factory or mill...
The paving-man leans on his two-handed rammer
—the reporter's lead flies swiftly over the
note-book...
The conductor beats time for the band, and all the
performers follow him,
The city sleeps and the country sleeps,
The living sleep for their time....the dead sleep for their time....
And these one and all tend inward to me, and I
tend outward to them,
And such as it is to be of these, more or less, I am.*

These lines appear in a long catalog of characters early in Whitman's
1855 *Song of Myself*. They're part of a dazzling but realistic tour of
American landscapes, times, and more than anything people. His
characters span the social spectrum, practice every occupation, and
live in all historical moments of U.S. history. As tour guide,
Whitman's narrating I/eye assumes what his people assume. He traps

muskrats with them, marries across race lines, eats, drinks, and stares deeply into an ox's eyeballs. His curiosity and heart are endless. The model American vitalist, Whitman's energy is boundless. He leaves nothing and no one alone.

The poet's massive affection is emotional and sexual, musical and material. Love is a binding balm that brings together elements strung taut in political as well as erotic tension. He sings of his beloved America on the verge of splitting apart along many different fault lines: between north and south, nationalism and states' rights, labor and management, women and men, the you of otherness and the I of identification and unity.

Singing up these angry pairs, Whitman had them fall in love with each other. It was his way of trying to save the land from the dreadful war soon to come and which many of his generation could see straight ahead, like a hurricane coming right at them. As editor for *The Brooklyn Daily Eagle*, Whitman took it upon himself to compose an editorial in 1847 in support of proposed legislation to ensure California and other territories taken with the Mexican War would enter the Union as free states. The editorial made no bones about it—Whitman was for free soil.

For this he was fired. *The Eagle's* owner, allied with the conservative wing of the Democratic party and reluctant to speak directly against the extension of slavery in the new territories, wouldn't tolerate his editor speaking out so definitively against the institution. Burned by this, Whitman gave up political writing. Instead, he spent his time writing poems, most of them not so promising. But by 1855, he'd loosened his hand enough to write the first edition of his magnificent *Song of Myself*. And he'd had visionary experiences like the one described in section 5:

> *Swiftly arose and spread around me the peace*
> *and joy and knowledge that pass all the art*
> *and argument of the earth,*
> *And I know that the hand of God is the promise*
> *of my own,*
> *And I know that the spirit of God is the brother*
> *of my own,*
> *And that all the men ever born are also my brothers, and the women my*
> *sisters and lovers,*

And that a kelson of the creation is love,
And limitless are leaves, stiff or drooping in the
fields,
And brown ants in the little wells beneath them,
And mossy scabs of the worm-fence, heaped stones,
elder, mullen, pokeweed.

Following a lyrically erotic encounter between the speaker and some unnamed other on a "transparent" June morning, these lines celebrate for the first time the resonant power of the poet's strong, meaty love. They also show off his recently achieved poetic ability. Suddenly he's not only competent. He's great.

The writings that make up this volume take Whitman's *Song of Myself* as a point of inspiration and departure. "He most honors my style who learns under it to destroy the teacher," Whitman writes near the end of his poem. The writers of *Songs of Ourselves* honor the poet's style by breaking the mold. What you'll find here doesn't refer openly to Whitman, but in many places it sounds like him—like his generous curiosity about his own embodied self and others, like his affection reciprocated or thwarted, like his adventurous mental wanderings in lands around the globe. The America the writers here sing of isn't Whitman's America by any means. The contributions to *Songs of Ourselves* often show the ironic turns away from the ideal unities Walt Whitman imagined. But each of them in its own way voices a self that belongs in one of *Song of Myself's* many long lists of characters. Each sings her own song of life in the twentieth century and the millennium.

Songs of Ourselves is saturated in what Whitman called amity—a love that's platonic and fraternal and at times romantic at the edges. This great affection is one of the binding features of the widely varying "songs" presented here. Susan Lee Feathers mourns the loss of her beloved sister at the same time she bemoans the devastation of the marine environment of the Gulf in the 2010 Deep Water Horizon explosion. Peter W. Fong sings his affection for the "lane teem[ing] with the life of the suburbs" of Mumbai. G. Bruce Boyer shows amused tenderness for his fellow captives and benign captors in the hospital psychiatric ward. The pained affection in Paul Heller's voice narrates with great sympathy the troubles of Albert, T, L, and the little hoodlum Matthew in downtown Allentown. Raymond M. Wong is lovingly baffled at his father's distant silence after his family leaves China. G. B. Miller gives us his bottomless affection for the life of the theatre. Tomas Benitez describes his Boyle Heights, LA home with deep devotion, and he carries on amiable exchanges with his old friends, the animals of the gully. Sherry Stratton makes herself part of the family of birds and deer in her suburban back yard. From microbes to the "Big Idea" of God, Donna Vitucci sings up a transcendentalist's vision of her complex America. Ann Sonz Matranga, Morton J. Miller, Patricia Wellingham-Jones, and Nancy Canyon conjure poignant tenderness for family members drifting out of reach. Linda Marsh tells a tale of parenting redolent with affection for her young children. Victoria Franzese invokes Allen Ginsberg, Whitman's poetic grandson and a great lover of New York, to sing up the ordinary times of a New York City mother. With his big band, Judith Farmer Miller's beloved father performs the special list of tunes demonstrating his idea that everybody has their song.

Landscape's powerful push and pull on the self, a central dynamic to Walt Whitman's writing, is another binding feature in several pieces here. Jim Brega takes us on a tour of upper Midwest cities, where as he tersely puts it "overall effect is that Armageddon happened and smokers were the only ones spared," but Frank Lloyd Wright's organic architecture has more salient effects. The cluttered cities of Tom Carter's Amazonian journey call for an intense focus on logistics and bureaucratic details that's only released when the voyagers finally get into the open jungle. Freddi Tachman Carlip sees beauty where "others see the wilderness" in the disorder of her farmhouse in an otherwise precisely groomed Pennsylvania suburb. Gail Reitano's New Jersey pine barrens give meaningful background to family history and the story of an Italian-American girlhood.

Good humor, one of Whitman's primary values, connects several of the contributions. Mary Flood's speaker specializes in an obsession that grows ever more hilarious as she complains of all the bad drivers on her daily travels—people who should know better and be safer for themselves and each other. Pamela Varkony takes us to a "Metaphysical Expo," where the crystals, tarot readings, and angels of many shapes for sale promise the "manifestation of desire;" meanwhile ranks of golf carts stand as "testament to the lure of the unknown." Nicholas DiGiovanni imagines his "still young and beautiful corpse... sitting up" at his own memorial service. The corpse smokes, wears a bemused smile, and shocks mourners when he opens his mouth to say "welcome to my funeral."

The U.S. pictured in many of these writings has fallen far away from the sweet amigo world of Whitman's dreams. Still, they carry on his vitalist energy and his generous spirit. A friend reminded me the other day that although he's never really grown up he's pretty sure he's grown older. If Walt Whitman finally did grow old (and die!) his work has never really grown up—not in the sense of settling down to a single understanding or stable and steady meaning. It's constantly being reimagined, as the contributions to *Songs of Ourselves* give luminous evidence.

If you want to find Walt, take his advice and look for him under the boot soles of these songs, where he sprouts fresh from the grass, and differently.

SUSAN LEE FEATHERS

Caretta caretta...No, It's Not a Song, It's a Symphony

Curves

I drive to Santa Rosa Island over the Escambia Bay Bridge on the Gulf Coast near Pensacola, Florida. It is very early in the morning. The sand is so white it appears as snow drifts. I am mystified, scoop it up and fill a vial to send to friends in the desert I left behind.

Walking past dunes, out onto the shore, I feel my spirit lighten. For the first time I see the curve of the planet on the horizon where the cobalt sea touches the sky.

There are seabirds in clusters along the water and some dive for silvery fish that flap at the water's surface. Crabs dart in and out of tunnels near the shoreline, perching with beady eyes in my direction, ready to plunge out of sight as I approach.

Men and women fish from shore, and some are waist deep, heaving heavy lines to snag the Bonita they tell me are running. Dolphins dive into a circle of bubbles for the day's catch in a time and place where I begin a journey from desert to sea, the curve of my horizon.

Passages and Oil Spills

The Deep Water Horizon platform explodes on April 20, 2010, killing 11 people and releases crude oil in a torrent into the Gulf of Mexico. In a nearby hospital, my sister struggles on life support to recover from open heart surgery, performed a month before the explosion. At night, I email family about Beverly's decline while I

6

watch news about the approaching oil spreading across the Gulf coastal waters. Pensacola waits in grim anticipation as we do.

Beverly dies on April 27 at 3:43 PM. Over the 53 days of her struggle, she navigates terrifying medical procedures, tubes, drains, trachs and vents, and dialysis machines. We watch my sister's body swell beyond belief, turn red and raw; we gently kiss the scabs and bruises on her arms that crust and ooze with edema. On her last day, the sheets are soaked from her body fluid.

It is one week now. Her body is cremated. Jenny gives her mother a wonderful memorial. When friends and family leave for home, I feel emotional numbness like petrification.

Meantime the oil continues to billow into the Gulf, so loved by my sister, creeping toward the beach on which she watched green-glass seas lap against snow-white sand.

The Gulf lies as Beverly did—helpless to inevitable disaster—concerned people all around who cannot prevent it. I walk the shores weeping for Bev even as I weep for dolphins and schools of silver pompano, and the microbial hordes whose haven will soon confront a wrath.

I know what it is to feel totally helpless.

I grew up on Route 66

I grew up on Route 66. Daughter of a military officer, my gyroscope was set to travel over hill and dale until one night dad announces, "Take down the wallpaper! We've got orders!"

Somewhere on a dark, winding road, my arms propped on the dashboard, listening to tales my father weaves about his boyhood in rural Tennessee—somewhere under that theater of stars and drone of wheels on Route 66—I fell in love with America.

My gyroscope bent toward Southerners, Yankees, Mid-Westerners, Californians, Hawaiians, Native Americans, hicks and sophisticated New Yorkers, hillbillies and coal miners.

Yet I put down no roots of my own. I floated above the earth in limbo. I was a gypsy girl who knew a lot about other people but little about herself. Later, I would begin to search for "me" in the open space of democracy.

For many decades I believed that people who lived in one place all their lives had an advantage over drifters like me. I guess I still do, but I can now see that living in many regions of the U.S. gave me something my place-bound friends did not have: the range of experiences being an American means. I owe the military life for spurring a sense of belonging to the whole nation.

I've never had a regional viewpoint or felt that one landscape was more valuable than another. So, I sing my song, the song of this land over which I continue to move.

That Room

On Selfridge Air Force Base, a row of stately houses lines a circular field. I walk across a white expanse from where my friends and I have just built an igloo in the depth of a Michigan winter.

My boots crunch up the snow-encrusted steps to the heavy door. I can see a roaring fire through the sheer window-drapes on the adjacent windows.

I am delighted to discover my father with his pipe and paper, relaxing before a fire. Overhead, a chandelier throws rainbows on the green rug. A snoozing gold collie and gray cat are the heaving lumps before the fire.

"The Abominable Snowman!" Dad exclaims. I giggle and fall into his lap, crushing the newspaper. He smells of sweet tobacco and coffee. A few minutes later he returns to read and I slither down onto the rug, and loll with dog and cat, before the fire.

Mom's distant voice calls from the kitchen, "Girls, girls, fudge is ready!" My big sister appears to organize, as she always does. There will be warm fudge, cold milk, and a round of Monopoly.

We gather at the card table set near the warmth of the fire. My little sister is standing at the window pointing with her plump, baby hand at the snowflakes twirling out of the cold night.

The room by now is warm through and through, the dog has turned on its back to air its hairy underside and the cat is missing. Dad scrapes the bowl of his pipe, refills and lights it with a flourish. He walks to the radio, gives the dial a solid turn, leans down with his ear tuned to the wheezing and cracking high-pitched whine. The Green Hornet and Kato are on the trail again.

The Human Condition

My father is 94, still going strong. Last night, over our mid-week dinner conversation, he extols what his generation accomplished in the 1940s.

"I wish we had a vision like that again," he laments.

He describes a national vision of America's destiny, the shared feeling that together the nation could accomplish something great for the whole world. He remembers that nations looked to America to make things right.

The second thing Dad says is, "You just can't change American's love affair with their cars." We are talking about reducing carbon emissions in the U.S.

I try to imagine the sea change for his generation—from horse and buggy to a gas-powered vehicle, from oil lamps to electricity—how his world transformed as ours does with the Internet and wireless devices.

Yet, any similarities between Dad's lifetime and mine end there. The geopolitical, corporate society which dominates our lives poses a different breed of foe than Hitler and his minions. We are our own enemy—a promise and a challenge. The way now is inward to meet the challenges of a new time and reality.

Still, I spend time with Dad to understand how his experience might inform mine. I spend time with Dad because I love the stories of families gathered on the front porch after dinner. I listen as he describes his angst at living in a small rural town, wishing to explore the world beyond it.

I see in his experience the age-old struggle of the human condition: the individual need for freedom versus the benefits of the "tribe."

Maybe, I think, we really aren't so different.

Passing of the Chief

On December 7, Pearl Harbor Day, our father, Edward B. Feathers, passed away peacefully in his easy chair at home.

Known to his family and close friends as Chief Talking Bear in honor of his loquacious online presence, Dad proceeded to draw together a Family Council. He named each member of his tribe: Morning Star, Laughing Waters, Bluebird, He-Who-Digs, Little Eagle, and so on. Daughters, grandchildren, and the daughters of his flight crew, made up the circle.

Each day Dad quoted poetry and invited council members to send their favorites. My sister Kathy inherited his gift for reciting poetry, and the two of them entertained us for years.

9

These are the regular, simple things he did for us, that kept us all together and nourished our souls as we were out in the world with all its "slings and arrows of misfortune."

We loved our father—this man of deep emotions, rarely shown—of constant and steady love, and a bit of the rascal mixed in to keep the balance. He had a profound influence on each of our lives.

As each day passes beyond his military burial—please accept this flag from a grateful nation—we are more aware of how much his life supported and enriched our own.

Deer Springs Inn

Deep ruts rock the car as we make our way on a forest road lined by Ponderosa, spruce, and juniper stands. Deer Springs Inn is a place so special that word of mouth is its only marketing.

We hear the sharp bugle of bull elk nearby. The owners make a fire with resinous wood, and give us sticks for roasting marshmallows. With the dark of the woods surrounding us, faces light-up in the yellow flames. Through the arms of towering pines, a circle of stars glitters white.

Days turn into a week. Tom and Heather sketch and write in the cabin's journal where guests record their experiences. We enjoy turning back pages to learn how other families discovered the woods, campfire, and friends. Some write poems or include a bird feather.

This year we stay at Bounding Bear cabin, before that Silver Squirrel, until by the time we all leave Arizona, the Williams will have slept in every cabin. Sometimes we bring friends, but mostly it is just the three of us. It is our place of repose.

In 2012, the Rodeo-Chedisky Fire burns a half million acres of forest including Deer Springs Inn. The diaries go up in flames – poems, drawings, anecdotes, and memories incinerated.

It is a "hot" fire that destroys the potential for germination of seeds. The forest must be replanted. Deer Springs Inn is rebuilt. Young saplings grow and bright green meadows appear among blackened stumps.

Gone are the mature wood, the elk, deer, owls, and creatures that animate it. The beauty of this world is fragile and fleeting.

Journey Home

My grown children are excited to return to the home of their youth. The little pond across the road reminds Tom and Heather of ice skating with friends. On icy, cold days the waitress at the diner, where we are drinking steaming mugs of chocolate and eating greasy burgers, tells us the pond remains unfrozen now.

In 1972, my husband and I move to Croton-on-Hudson, N.Y. with a 2 yr-old son and infant daughter. The first winter in the little hamlet of 6,000 residents, snow piles up around our door and blankets streets shutting down schools and making the commute to New York a trek with uncertain outcome. More than once my husband sleeps on the train, mired in drifts.

Living in Croton we played in winter. Every pond and stream freezes solid. During the cold, snowy months I read books to Tom and Heather in the cozy dormer of our Cape Cod house. Lacey snowflakes drift past the windows framed by frost.

But THAT Croton, we learn is no more. Absence of a quarter century allows us to see the dramatic changes in climate and landscape. Young families living there look at us like we are talking about Vermont or Alaska. Our home sits at the edge of a golf course and expensive homes. The woods where deer crept into our yard and large maples and elms stood over elegant dogwoods are all gone, and with them the little brook that my daughter frequented, sitting on an old stone wall of a century past.

Places

My family history begins in the Smoky Mountains where I was born at the end of WWII, when my father, a native of east Tennessee, returned to the States. I was whisked into 16 crazy years of military assignments that took my family from coast to coast with one magical time in Hawaii.

Changing places frequently lends to a sense of loss and confusion precisely for the reasons that place is not a location but is the font of our biological and psychological lives. I am only now beginning to appreciate this phenomenon, now looking back, and frankly savoring all the rich, diverse places on my "dance card" in life.

I believe that as a child I innately understood this essential relationship and became a great explorer of natural places, lithe and intentional about getting to know each new place. From laying on my tummy watching the miniature world of grass forests to the thrill of rolling down a leaf covered hill letting the Earth pull me to her breast—I longed for that intimate attachment.

Caretta caretta...no, it's not a song, it's a symphony.

Caretta caretta doesn't even know we've tagged her with a dichotomous name to set her species apart from others. Her only inclination is to find a darkened shoreline and lay her burden down. She paddles with strong legs through the warm current, navigating by a magnetic field. The moonlit shore is quiet as she takes purchase on the sand below her.

Every May through September, female loggerhead turtles return to lay their eggs in the dunes of their birth. As I walk, I am mindful to look for what appears to be the tread marks of a truck tire. If I should walk after dark, and I am very lucky, I might see her high on the dune line, digging in her lumbering way.

Caretta caretta spent her youth in the Sargasso Sea, where she grows under the protective cover of sargassum weed. When she comes of age, dozens of eggs will grow within her as she heads back to the same beach where as a hatchling she fought her way to the shoreline under the gaze and jabs of shorebirds, the clutches of ghost crabs, and fangs of night predators.

One of a few to survive to adulthood, she now returns to lay down the next generation. Of seven species of sea turtles in the world, four lay their eggs here at the beach on which I wander —a biological treasure.

The First American Democracy

In 1990 I sought to learn about America's First Nations. I left a high profile position, gave away my possessions, packed my truck, and traveled to a dusty border town, trusting my inner compass.

There a man and woman agreed to take me as a student. My internal landscape was at war. I had come to the realization I was living a lie. I remember the unreality of my life as I drove to work where architecturally beautiful buildings and the expansive green of a golf course tumbled down to the deep blue of the Pacific Ocean. Contrary to the beauty of the surroundings, I spent my days administering programs for patients wrecked on the shoals of the American Dream.

I remember that day when I sat in my office on a singing blue-sky day feeling uninspired. My eyes settled on a book that lay unread: Touch the Earth (T.C. McLuhan). As I opened its cover, a profound sense of relief came over me. Reading the words of Native America's great leaders gave me the direction I sought. There was a pulsing hunger at my core for knowledge, like something lost and vaguely remembered.

The next three years living in the daily presence of two American Indian teachers changed the way I see myself and the world around me. I believe the experience made me a better person and a better American. But the path to self-understanding is a crucible where falseness is burned away and a tender new skin grown.

Synchronicities

I drive to San Diego for a brief stay at Rancho la Puerto, a spa and retreat center near Tecate, Baja California. Unbeknownst to me, the resort is on the grounds of a previous Essene community established in the 1940s. The library still shelves many of the community's books.

One evening, I discover the small library left from the early days there. There is a history of its founder Edmond Bordeaux Szekely, a translator and student of world religions.

The American Essene Community flourished for fifty years at Rancho La Puerto, and evolved into the present-day spa as visitors wanted to experience the quietude and spiritual practice.

Szekely is the scholar who translated the Essene Gospel of Peace from the original Aramaic, the native language of Jesus. He was given permission to translate the texts that were kept under lock and key in the Vatican. Szekely discovered he followed the path of St. Benedict who hid the texts in a time when extant writings were hidden or destroyed to fit the Pope's objectives.

These ancient documents precede the Dead Sea Scrolls of Qumran, and represent ancient teachings as old as eight thousand years before the current era.

I find a copy of the Essene Gospel and eagerly read these teachings. I am struck by the fact that the Gospel is similar to the Great Law of Peace of the Iroquois Confederacy. These synchronicities happen many times on my path of self-realization. I learn that knowledge is everywhere, if only a person seeks it.

TOMAS BENITEZ

The Gully

1.   Very quiet in the Gully tonight. Frigid air and a darkened sky. Even the Pomona Freeway Ocean seems subdued. A breeze slices across the yard, somehow adding to the stillness. I feel like I am being watched. I stare into the thicket under the yucca tree. It stares back at me, the darkness. The glow from my zippo flame, even for just a moment, betrays a pair of eyes, waiting, staring. Is it you Skunk? Am I being hunted? Skunks from East L.A. can be so thug.

2.   This is the Boyle Heights I grew up in. Mexicans from here and Mexicans from there, Jews, Japanese, a few Russians and the odd Black, White, Chinese or Italian family. We played baseball together. We worshipped differently, spoke the same language (and something else to our families), ate each other's food and lied to each other about what we knew about God, Commies, Sex and War. We watched the same TV programs, we had the same heroes, we had the same dreams, and we all wanted to play for that new baseball team in town, the Los Angeles Dodgers. I am very proud to be a Chicano, but the homogeny of East LA today is overrated. This is the kind of childhood that cures bigotry, ends ignorance and abates fear. I learned to appreciate my identity and respect other races from my folks, but I learned to live it from growing up with my pals and our neighborhood baseball team, The Evergreen Comets, champions of the whole world and everything else.

3.   The Gully calls me out of bed too early in the morn or too late in the night, a disjointed sleep; it happens. But there before me, out of the cold and dark, an old friend emerges from the thicket under the yucca tree. The Skunk saunters at first, and then upon

seeing me stops. I wait frozen. Too close to run for it. But then the Skunk turns and goes on his/her way. Ever see a Skunk walk by you while carrying an attitude? Not unlike the walk of shame, only with more sashay and panache. Staccato, bravado, but a little bit of allegro. The Skunk has made the point, we will share the territory. I have made mine and agree.

4.   Something about Sunday nights, a little sad, harkens to a time being driven back home from Dad's to Mom's. It was always late so I was just about getting back home to East LA for school the next day. I was always glad to be home but the quiet was often underwhelming. Mom would get up half asleep and open the door, thank Dad and get me to my room. A kiss and I was left to unpack and get ready for bed. Ever since then, me and Sunday nights have always been a little distant. The Gully senses this, I think, and sends me stars and La Luna, plus a nice breeze, not bitter, brisk. A message, "Get over yourself." The Pomona Freeway Ocean is also letting me know I'm not alone, with louder and steadier than usual rumbling waves. Maybe more cars filled with kids in the backseat being driven home. At least, standing out by the Gully, I am home.

5.   Like spotting an old girlfriend who looks better now than before—it's been a few days since I've had a chance to visit with the Gully and take in the comfort. It's Saturday night out there and lots of tinkling glasses, laughter and music, but here it is quiet that breeds solace. The steady gentle roaring of the Pomona Freeway Ocean, like listening to an animal breathe. Jinx is off chasing noises in the bushes, the half-light of La Luna shining just a bit of glow to the stars and outlining the trees.

6.   My Skunk has gone missing from the Gully. It is hard to put into words how one can come to miss a feral skunk, but I do. Maybe Skunk did not like the way I smell, or perhaps had a delayed reaction to my marking out my territory. Skunks are mother nature's temperamental teenager. Kind of like an Emo; they have the same hair. But I do miss the Skunk. I blame the Possums.

7.   Quietude in the Gully. No moaning animals or ruckus. It's as if the Pomona Freeway Ocean knows and slows to a steady

rocking heartbeat rhythm. The waves rumble with a distant peace. La Luna is framed by the dark outline of the palm fronds on the left, the Yucca tree on the right seems to be reaching up like a hand holding her aloft. She is so beautiful tonight; it is all about her I suspect. Maybe the animals are huddled in their shadowed hovels also watching her. Not even Jinx is dancing in her moonlight. We're in church.

8.   Rain in the early morning in the Gully brings the sweet smell of wet earth, and a glean to the leaves turning green as light takes over the day. But out on the Pomona Freeway Ocean I think I heard the sound of a nearby shipwreck. I pray that no one has been lost at sea. Keep an even keel folks; mind your sails and stay on a steady course.

9.   Saw a funny beautiful thing this afternoon. Out on the street, this old Mexican couple—the woman walking behind the man. Wait, just wait. But she was pushing him, like with a shove, and then he'd go forward a few steps, balance on the cane, and then she'd come up and push him again, and he'd go forward again. This is how they were taking a walk. And they were talking, not even about their routine; I think it was about food, maybe, but there they were, push, step step, stop. Push step step stop. Love.

11.   The Raccoon and I are not friends. One of us is a surly, quick-tempered wild beast, with big dark eyes, the other is a raccoon. But we are neighbors. Out in the Gully, the yard is a crossroads of animals, domestic and not; humans are only tolerated. Tonight the raccoon crosses the yard as I sit and watch the moon. He stops mid-trip and sits to look at me. I look back. Maybe he is reaching out to me? Or maybe he smells the onion rings I ate a short while before. Just as easily as he had stopped he calmly turns and continues on his way.

12.   Out in the Gully tonight it is as ever a quiet place for peaceful reflection. But, then a lesson takes place. Two Possums, one Larger, the other clearly Younger file across the yard, the Larger in the lead. He gets about halfway across my bow, suddenly stops, looks at me, thinks better of it and turns around. I'm slightly hurt, for I

offer no malice or harm in heart or mind. But then again, he is a Possum, and they do that. He turns back to where he came from and runs into a cactus in a planter, bumps off, and carries on. The Younger, following in the footsteps of the elder, also walks right into the same planter, bumps off, and carries on. This is why I will never be caught drunk in front of my son: they are always watching us.

13.   From my perch up above the Gully I can hear the pings off the bats as the last of the games and batting practices are wrapping up over at the nearby park. Music to my ears, but nothing sounds like wood on leather. If you've ever hit a ball as hard as you can with a wooden bat it makes a sound you remember the rest of your life. Still, it's baseball in barrio. It's a giant outdoor church, and it is good.

14.   Jose can you see the skies over the Gully tonight? Rockets' red glare and the bombs bursting in air, give proof through the night that East LA is still here! Hello, live from atop my intrepid perch somewhere in the war zone: fireworks. Next door, across the street, in the street, at the nearby park, the top of the hill, the bottom of the hill, all around us. The Pomona Freeway Ocean runs silently under the cacophony; the bushes are ripe with crouching figures, two eyes wide opened, waiting, hiding, and the air smells of carne asada and gunpowder. Smell that smell? I love the smell of the Fourth of July in the Eastside! Happy birthday America; let's grow on.

15.   Just got back in from saying goodnight to La Luna, thanked her for the moonbeams and good feeling she gives, even the little bit of craziness I get from her vibe; still feels good when she does that to me. Have you ever, really, actually danced under the moonlight? Maybe with somebody you loved, still love, maybe not loved, but was a lover? The song that was the song then will never leave you, never.

PETER W. FONG

Journal of Infectious Diseases

When traveling in Asia, I am sometimes struck by the union of blue and brown: blue American passport, tanned brown skin. Their convergence on my person allows me to cross borders with relative ease, to mingle in crowds like a distant cousin at a family reunion.

One afternoon in Mumbai, while I am walking alone and without destination, a white- robed itinerant rages toward me, waving his walking stick like a cudgel. Because I am the only other person in the near vicinity, I suppose I ought to be afraid. Before I can attain an appropriate state of fear, however, he is already past me, continuing to wield that stick, confronting an adversary I cannot see.

There was a time—as a childless couple in Missoula, Montana—when Sarah and I truly enjoyed going to bars. We would lean our bicycles against a downtown parking meter and, depending on our mood, proceed from the Rhino to the Iron Horse, from the Bodega to the Boardroom, from Charlie's to Al and Vic's. At the end of a summer evening, suitably primed, we would ride no-hands along the leafy streets, a trick that I was too stiff to perform sober. Since those years, we have changed and matured. We have children now, for example, as well as mortgages. Two of each.

The lane teems with the life of the suburbs: curbside hairdressers, betel vendors, short-haired dogs, children in their school uniforms. The ironwork displays multiple representations of the Sanskrit *om*.

The balconies are shaded by a tamarind tree, indifferently festooned with wayward kites. The building across the way bears the shingles of an advocate of the high court and a "maternity surgical home." Through the open windows, I can hear music, horns, shouts, the accelerating rasp of two-cycle engines, the raucous calls of crows. It is the end of January, and the air vibrates with falling leaves.

In India, my brother Cliff and I share a room at a grand hotel that—if you ignore the central air-conditioning, television, minibar, shower, and bath—is somehow reminiscent of our former family home, at the corner of Lake and Center Streets, in the village of Perry, New York. Maybe it's the two single beds, but more likely it's the two of us.

Cliff knows more than I will ever learn about any number of subjects—modernist furniture and architectural pottery, for example—but, by that strange calculus of time and family, I am still his older brother, still in possession of a few mysteries myself.

"So," he asks, as we drift side by side on the hotel's twin box springs, seven thousand miles from our former bedroom, "what happened that night the police brought you home?"

Late the next night, Cliff and I are walking in an ancient and predominantly Muslim quarter, drifting and surging with the tides of shoppers and shopkeepers in the bazaar. There are men pushing wooden carts laden with crates and boxes, porters bearing woven baskets atop their heads, teenagers murmuring into cell phones, smaller children crowded around stone basins of aquarium fish, a merchant demonstrating a wind-up Victrola to a crowd of men in dusty robes.

I feel like I can hear the sounds of centuries overlapping.

According to the *Journal of Infectious Diseases*, the most common reason for travel among tourists who contract cholera is—you guessed it—a visit with the relatives.

I've traveled alone and with family but this moment is different somehow, maybe because Cliff asks if I could ever have imagined that we would be walking together in this unusual place and I have to say no, this is beyond imagining on any sort of personal level. No individual mind could have predicted that we would find ourselves at a shop named Decent Corner, two Chinese-American brothers who last shared a bedroom in a town best known, if known at all, as the childhood home of Chester A. Arthur.

Living in close proximity with millions of striving people, I can't help but entertain the old questions of resemblance, advantage, and inequity. What if I'd been born to a family of peasant farmers? Or migrant laborers? To a mother who sells bootleg DVDS on a dusty bridge and a father who scavenges cardboard and Styrofoam in his bicycle cart?

Favored with the benefits of the American systems of economy, justice, and education, what have I made of myself? A bewildered onlooker.

On the shelf in Decent Corner, a brand of chocolate-covered almonds called "American Eagle Droppings," with a red-white-and-blue logo of the slyly grinning bird.

In mid-month we set out for Vermont, leaving Montana as parched as it has ever been in July, the rivers too warm to fish. We take with us our ice skates and our winter clothes, two bicycles, a turkey call, and a circular saw. Also our noisy, bent-tailed cat, fresh off the plane from China, who has become very much attached to Montana after just a few weeks of mouse-hunting in our ungrazed pasture. He mourns his loss daily, hours of low-and high-pitched keening, which reverberates from the car windows like the sufferings of souls in purgatory.

As artist-in-residence, I curate an exhibit at the Madison Museum: letters from three eras of Yellowstone visitors (on foot, by horse-drawn carriage, and by automobile), a range of writing implements from the quill pen to the laptop computer, and a display of photographs taken by a member of Calvin Coolidge's party, in 1927. I also write my own letters every day, to family and friends, and hang a different one on the wall each morning alongside the historical artifacts. It's fun to watch tourists come across the new letter amid the old ones, then glance around guiltily as they realize that the personal details they are reading correspond with a person who is living in the same moment as themselves. Twice my own letters are stolen from the museum, which I consider a gratifying critical response.

On a day off in Ulaanbaatar, suffering from a spectacular abscess on my back, I walk to the Gandan Monastery. Like many monasteries throughout Mongolia, it was partially destroyed during the Soviet era, its monks forced out of service, jailed, or killed. Its standing image of the Bodhisattva of Compassion—almost 90-feet tall, cast in copper, and covered with gold—was completed in 1996, a half-dozen years after the Soviet departure.

As a personal metaphor, an abscess takes the cake: a festering from within, a little haven of infection that your own body nurtures and grows. Slightly delirious with pain, I enter the Dechengalpa Datsan, where the monks await their noon meal. They sit on raised platforms, with their shoes attending faithfully behind them, a sundry assortment of sandals, athletic shoes, and cavalry boots.

In their chants I can hear a blend of the mature and the childish; some of the robed figures look as young as seven or eight. Each monk receives a flat oblong of bread on which is piled a package of cookies and another of candy, along with a layered procession of other small snacks. I watch, straight-backed on a low bench, neither famished nor grateful.

After living in Tokyo and Shanghai, our family knows how bizarre and attractive our American holidays can appear to other cultures. You dress up in costume and ask strangers for candy? And they smile when they give it to you? Happy Halloween indeed. There must be something characteristically American about the trust required to ask, and the generosity necessary to give. Not to mention the penchant for disguise and the taste for sweets.

"From where I sit," says the editor of a luxury travel magazine, "Mongolia now is almost cliché. Last summer, it seemed like everybody was going to Mongolia. The bar keeps getting higher." It does me no good to protest that our travels are not merely another set of indicators, social markers that enter our conversations for the purpose of conferring status, as if one could display an experience like a brand. In a culture where any voyage less exotic than Melville's *Typee* risks relegation to the lesser ranks of adventurers, the truly irrelevant among us must find our way, unaided, to other sorts of journeys. Nearer, slower. Less distant, less peculiar. Places both familiar and strange, to be enjoyed rather than consumed: around the corner, the end of the block, the top of the hill, the other side of the river.

The Vermont winter has been inconsistent so far, alternating freeze and thaw, but we are grateful for snow. I'd forgotten how pleasant it can be to watch the snow accumulate, sometimes slowly, sometimes not, as capricious as memory. Is it such a wonder that, when humans regard the world, they see themselves reflected in it?

Because we were never properly introduced, I called him "The Screamer." Nobody else paid any attention to the guy, who stood facing the Yellow Sea, bellowing a full-throated challenge to the dawn. With his mouth closed, he would have been just another member of the early-morning crowd—the women in one-piece tank suits and bathing caps, the men in nylon briefs—most of them over fifty years old and exhibiting no concern with either the chilly October temperatures or the American obsession with body image. They fished, swam, jogged, played volleyball, practiced gymnastic routines. While he screamed. I'm sure there was a reason for all the shouting, but I couldn't muster enough Mandarin to ask.

The four of us lean our backs against the bank of a dry ditch and gaze into the blue skies above Montana's Treasure County. We don't have to look for geese, since they are everywhere. Canada geese, with their white cheeks and raucous voices. Bane of golf course groundskeepers and balm to the earth-bound, to all those who find solace in such grand evidence of the migratory urge. Some geese rise from the Yellowstone and fly purposefully over the beets and the corn. Some leave the fields and make for the river.

Others seem merely to be wandering from one gravel bar to the next, one farm furrow to another.

A New Yorker by birth but not by temperament, I've now traveled twice to Singapore since December, following an absence of more than a decade. Drawn back by food and family, of course, and in our family it's hard to know which comes first. One dish I won't forget is *ayam buah keluak*, chicken with Indonesian black nuts. Both flavor and texture are reminiscent of a Mexican mole, but the nuts are distinctively oily and addictively fragrant, like some strange combination of a truffle and a brazil nut. One online source reports that "The dusty grayish seeds . . . have already been treated to remove the poisonous effects by being thoroughly washed and boiled, then buried in the ground with layers of ash, banana leaves, and earth for forty days." That would explain a lot—about anything, or anyone.

Which reminds me of a recipe from my time as a fishing guide in the Florida Keys. Catch six conchs and pack them overnight in crushed ice. After the grip on the shell loosens with the chill, pull the animal free. Trim away the guts and peel off the skin. Dice the conch meat into a punchbowl along with two sweet onions, two green peppers, and a quart of cherry tomatoes. Season the mix with cilantro and jalapeños and cover with fresh lime juice. Refrigerate for at least several more hours, or as long as you can stand it.

Last week's newspaper contains an interesting story about the mainland Chinese fascination with mixed-race children. Or perhaps it is more about the protectiveness of American parents in foreign lands. After reading the piece several times, I'm still not sure. The writing appears thoughtful but its judgments are hidden in plain view.

Our family has encountered similar situations over the years—
Chinese tourists who ask to have their picture taken with us,
Nepalese porters who can't resist patting our daughter on the head—
but I'd never attributed this attraction to the mix in races.

It's always painful to leave Montana, even under a spring
snowstorm that slickens the interstate with a wash of cold gurry, a
crystalline mix of sand and salt and ice that freezes in a dark rime on
the truck: stalactites on the fenders, pinwheels on the lug nuts. What
I see on my journey east are sandhill cranes in the pale sky, antelope
and mule deer in the whitened fields, streamers of cloud trailing from
the gleaming peaks of the Crazies.

Five days later, having successfully navigated the hazards of Bad
Route Road (Montana), Motley (Minnesota), and the 8614-foot long
Mackinac Bridge (Michigan), I find the hills of Vermont newly green.
Bloodroot blooms along the brook and, beneath the beeches, a red
trillium.

On the one occasion when race came to mind, the attention we
received was far from benign. The incident occurred in Tagbilaran,
the so-called "city of peace and friendship" on the Philippine island
of Bohol. I didn't see it coming, nor did I see what happened as it
occurred. I heard Sarah cry out, and I followed her shocked gaze to
her attacker. The woman was not much more than five feet tall, with
streaks of gray in her black hair, and sun-weathered skin nearly the
same color as my own. She had used her clenched fist to deliver a
low blow, and now she stood glaring at us. There was a challenge in
her expression, along with something like hate, or defiance.

"What was that about?" I asked inanely, but the woman did not
respond. Meanwhile, Sarah had grabbed our son by the hand and
started across the street.

"Come *on*," she said. "Don't confront her."

I picked up our daughter and followed.

The geese wheel and call above us. Some flighty birds leave their
family groups for another flock, mortally inconstant. Their relatives
try to call them back, and so do we. Despite some practice, our

honking varies in its authenticity. To my ears, it is sometimes sickly, sometimes strident, sometimes insincere. Indifferent geese pass far overhead.

Indignant geese circle provokingly low, then fly off. But the indiscriminate cup their wings to alight—and we greet them with fire.

We flee several blocks in the general direction of our hotel, then slip into the friendly confines of a Chinese restaurant. One wall displays a banner congratulating local students, and several celebratory dinners are already in progress. Over the family plates of comfort food (roast duck and pan-fried shrimp), Sarah and I try to decipher what this incident means. But we can't. There had been no identifiable provocation. The woman did not have the unfettered look of a lunatic, and yet she had acted purposefully, with malice aforethought. The explanation that I do not want to consider is racial hatred. Had the woman looked first at my tanned hide, then at Sarah's white skin? Had she contemplated our children's post-ethnic features before striking at the offending womb? After all, such a reaction would not have been inconceivable in North America, within our parents' memories. As recently as 1950, fifteen states—including Montana, Maryland, and California—prohibited marriage between whites and Asians.

If I say it one more time, maybe I'll convince myself: Sarah and I like Montana, and our house, and the people there. The townsfolk trust you to pump your gas before you pay. That's no small thing—in Boston and Los Angeles we grew accustomed to paying first, to the grave assumption of dishonesty that implies. And yet we continue to leave. Is this due to some grave defect in character? Or are we nomadic by nature? According to the U.S. Census Bureau, the average American packs his duffel a dozen times before he finds that final resting place. My own parents moved nearly every summer during my elementary years. By the time I reached ninth grade I'd been enrolled in seven different schools: urban, rural, Midwestern, public, private, Catholic, Lutheran. Sarah's father was a diplomat, then an international banker. She'd seen New York, London, Paris, and Helsinki by age twelve. Before she became a teacher, she sold airline tickets to college students. If the kids had money to spare, Sarah encouraged them to go far, to stay away as long as they could.

Perhaps it's understandable that, when September comes, our pinfeathers itch. We get half a mind to ramble. We fall into motion like flat stones skipping across a pond, or those songbirds that rise and fall in their flights across fields. We descend, struggle to regain the air, finally touch down. This behavior threatens even our mundane choices—so that the question becomes not only "Where should we live?" or "Where could we be happy?" but also "Where should we go for breakfast?"

I have been home from Mongolia for a month now, enough time to cut some firewood, find a new job, and participate in a presidential election—the most gratifying, by far, of the eight in which I've had the hard luck to vote. We spent the previous two debacles abroad— in Japan, then China—feeling disconnected if not actually disenfranchised, so it was hard to shake off that uncertain sense of doom, the fear of going to bed whole and waking up in fractions, unrecountably diminished.

In June, looking north from Vermont's Mount Ascutney, I really didn't know what I was seeing. There were trees with leaves, trees with names that are hardly mentioned in Montana: beech, ash, oak, and hornbeam. From above, the landscape looked cozy and inhabited, with quilted patches of woodlot and pasture. It was a pleasant perspective, without the constant reproach of "No Trespassing" signs that I experience on the ground here. I've been spoiled by Montana's 32 million acres of public land—more than five times the area of the entire state of Vermont. An unfair comparison, I know, but consider these additional statistics: public land accounts for almost 35 percent of Montana, but only 8 percent of Vermont. No wonder I feel hemmed in.

The twenty-first president of the United States, nicknamed the Gentleman Boss, Chester A. Arthur succeeded to the post after

James Garfield's assassination. By most accounts, he was a better statesman than anyone had the right to expect. Even the deservedly cynical Mark Twain admitted that, "It would be hard indeed to better President Arthur's administration." It was during his term that Congress first passed the Chinese Exclusion Act (1882). Immigrants of Chinese descent would remain ineligible for U.S. citizenship until 1943.

One odd thing about dislocation as a way of life is the whirlpool of memory. Whenever I am tempted to consign the past to a predictable current, like an oarsman on a favorite river, or to a periodic ebb and flow, as comforting as the tides, the gyre returns, spinning.

And so the air is warm as breath again, with the faint hint of frangipani that we loved in Thailand and Malaysia. And there are geckos here too, but the locals call them pega pega instead of chee chak. Like us, they are not natives to Aruba, but transplanted foreigners who have embraced their new home.

Our street is named after an obscure French author and alcoholic, Alfred de Musset, who did not die soon enough to escape Rimbaud's assessment of him as constitutionally incapable of true "vision." Here, at least, he intersects with Byron, is only two blocks shy of Victor Hugo, and resides within shouting distance of Shakespeare. Surely that is consolation, if consolation there might be.

Across the way, our neighbors fly a flag printed with the image of a yellowfin tuna and keep noisy parrots on the patio. Which reminds me both of the Maldives and of my first island home in Florida, where two of my dearest friends served a nightly highball to their Chihuahua.

For years I've had a recurring dream that takes place in an old museum of natural history. Not one of the new and shiny temples to technology, but a musty building with wooden staircases, peeling paint, and open windows. As it turns out, this place exists: in Shanghai's former Cotton Exchange building, built in 1923. As befits a dreamscape, I share the dinosaur bones, Neolithic dioramas, and jars of snakes in preservative with numerous groups of shuddering schoolgirls, all of us marveling at the stuffed whale shark suspended in front of aqua blue curtains, and—discreetly sequestered in a second-floor gallery—two deadpan mummies, chastely draped.

Flaubert argues that there are only three requirements for happiness: selfishness, stupidity, and good health. "Though if stupidity is lacking," he said, "all is lost." I am happy to listen to the Red Sox score five runs in the bottom of the eighth, so there's hope for me.

While dragging the kayak up the sand on Sunday, I meet a man from Venezuela who has been coming to Aruba since the mid-1970s. In those days, he used to fish in the October tournaments sponsored by the local yacht clubs. He participated every year until 1995, when one of his best friends had a heart attack on the boat and died. We agree that there are worse ways to go; even so, he doesn't have to explain why he now fishes from the beach.

In the twenty years since his friend's death, the man has caught only two fish. He sees them swim by—jacks, bonefish, snook—and he casts for them, but whether he catches them or not is unimportant to the experience.

As it turns out, he landed the second fish just last week: a snook that topped thirty pounds on the scale his wife uses to weigh their luggage. A young couple pointed the fish out to him as it cruised along the beach. "Is that the kind you're trying to catch?" they asked. The fight took him at least a hundred paces north, then south again, scattering bathers and drawing a small crowd. (Aruba being a friendly place, I actually heard about the fish on the day it was landed.) Somehow, he and the snook managed to avoid all the arms, legs, buoys, and other obstacles that might have intervened. When the leader finally snapped—with the fish within arm's reach of the sand—the snook was too tired to swim away.

"It was," the man said, "my time."

PAUL HELLER

Summer in the Rust Belt

On my way back to Allentown, just outside the Holland Tunnel I stop at the Tunnel Diner for coffee. Use the men's room on the way out to my truck, no wall between the urinal and hopper, leg to leg with a constipated Chinaman.

Visit the liquidator Dave Fox. Nothing I'm interested in buying. Fox's currently auctioning off an avalanche of dot.coms. Gets a read on the owners by how closely their offices resemble playpens. The greedy juveniles paid themselves huge salaries and left the investors to eat the hit. Then they show up at auction and buy back their stuff for pennies on the dollar. It's like the twenties, in and out and set for life at 30, stocks and land and avarice.

Queer for blueberries. Elias Fruit Market at Front and Tilghman, on the edge of the old Syrian neighborhood. Family manned, low overhead, selling no name produce and Middle Eastern essentials for a song. It teems. Pakistani women in headdress, spandexed Puerto Ricans, edgy Blacks, Asians in western garb, old-fashioned Germans in gingham; workers continuously re-stocking iced shelves from dripping crates.

At summer camp in Maine, they let us roam unsupervised through the high fields above the main lodges. My friends and I lay on the ground amidst the bushes and gorged till our bellies bloated. And now late July, blueberries from the south Jersey berry plains, from the bluette fields of Quebec. When the price falls from an early season high of almost $3 a box to as low as 99 cents a box, I strike, buying half a dozen boxes a week. I bury my morning cereal in them. Eat them by the handful through the day. A head, a freak, I am not ashamed.

At an outdoor house auction I spot a tall Mennonite boy who's stepped out of a Thomas Hart Benton painting. He's wearing black work pants held up by suspenders, dusty black work boots, a short-sleeved white shirt, and a small straw hat. His eyes a bright alert blue, his nose like a hawk's, his cheeks shine like cherries. Toward the end of the auction, three teenage boys ride up on bikes. One of them has punk green hair and rings in his nose and ears. He's wearing baggy shorts that fall to his calves and a MegaDeath sweatshirt. He exudes nihilism. I want to photograph these two boys from different planets standing together but can't. The Mennonites don't tolerate being treated as curiosities and I don't have a long distance lens.

Three bikers from the Bethlehem chapter of the Pagans work for me as furniture strippers. No nonsense boys, they arrive on Harleys, do their work, leave. Their Code is old fashioned, time honored: beer and angel dust to the duelist's champagne but with the same range of things offensive and the same solution. Today a fine death should the situation demand it.

Should one avoid these situations at any cost?

Never, says the Kamikazi. I am but one on an endless strand of pearls.

Always, says Falstaff. There is nothing to be gained by dying.

The lead biker T is one of the gang's enforcers, part Slav, part American Indian, jet hair, mastodon shoulders and arms, has all his teeth, a presence. Sometimes half a dozen Pagans arrive, the roar of their bikes bouncing off the warehouse overhang. I tell T the protocol: no coke, no rough stuff, no pissing behind the dumpster, no grabbing at my girl sanders' tits.

Friday. Payday. At lunch break, Albert, one of my finishers, asks me for his paycheck, has to pick up something for the weekend. Trots off, he doesn't have a car. Half an hour later he's back, eyes red-rimmed. Tells me he cashed his paycheck, walked to Pine Street, handed 200 in twenties to a street weed dealer—this is how he always scores—street guy goes into a row-house, doesn't come back out. My guy bangs on the front door. A different guy answers. Has no idea what Albert's talking about.

I call T over. He shakes his head as Albert recounts his tale of woe. Albert could have asked T for what he wanted—the Pagans are major players in the trade—but like most of the men who work for me Albert is afraid of him.

T knows the Pine Street setup, tells Albert he'll see what he can do. With my permission of course, he'll be gone for a while. He leaves on his Harley, Ace a second Pagan riding shotgun. Two hours later they're back. T nods at me, says something to Albert, and he and Ace go back to work. Ten minutes later my cell phone rings. A scared voice tells me he'll return the money and give an ounce on the house to Albert, but only after T's shift is over, when is that? We stop at 4:30 I tell him. He'll come at 5. Albert and I are sitting on the loading dock, a beat up black Ford pulls up, three guys in it. One gets out, hands Albert a wad of bills and a bag of weed, gets back in the car and goes.

The next morning I ask T, How? He explains that he went to high school with the Pine Street jefe Jacko's sister Maria. Had a thing with her. He goes to Maria's house, she's home. He explains the situation to her, tells her to get word to Jacko that if this isn't fixed before dark he'll come back and burn the house down with her in it.

My warehouse is bare storage so I have a small office a few blocks away in L's upholstery factory. L, just returned from Cozumel, had his left ear pierced. I smirk at this addition to his physiognomy as I pass him in the factory hallway. He says he was very drunk and woke up on the beach tender-lobed with no idea how or why. Then immediately, he says he was kidding, that he wasn't drunk at all and that his wife and friends encouraged him and approved. He storms into his office, slamming the door, furious that I had made him make excuses. L rigidly refuses to be moved from any position he's chosen to take. It's easier just to be belligerent, no arguing. Most people don't push back. Because I do, our working relationship is laced with unease.

In late June stumbling through the dune grass in Barnagat, L was bitten by a tick. He developed Ehrlichia. His temperature shot up to 103 and he spent four miserable days in a hospital. On his first day back at work, weak and heavily medicated, he was tranquil and accessible, a rational L, an L as he should be. Unfortunately, after two days the medicine kicked in.

When they see the gold earring in L's ear, his Syrian landlord A and his two younger brothers go into culture shock. A pulls me into the stairwell. A real man doesn't pierce his ears, he says, as his younger brothers nod agreement. We thought we knew L. Would I please explain.

Landlord A arrived from Syria twenty years ago. He's a minor American mullah. He considers women chattel. In exchange for a home they must breed sons and pretty marriageable daughters. When he felt secure enough to breed, A returned to his native village in Syria for a wife and procured a beauty. She's provided him with two daughters and two sons so he is batting 500. All of them, to their good fortune, look like his wife. A is adamantly against community property. Should he die suddenly, he says, his worth should go to his sons or revert to his two brothers. In India until recently, I tell him, a wife threw herself on her husband's funeral pyre. A good custom, he says.

On Monday, I spoke to Mitch—L's shop steward—in the men's room. I asked how he was feeling. Not so hot. He looked a sunken whisper of his venomous self. He was late forties and still lacerated his body with booze and pills but couldn't dish out a beating or satisfy a stripper. As shop steward he was hemmed in by spics and slants who wanted to work not strike. He was diabetic. Divorced. Had two children he never saw. Didn't have a girlfriend. His prized pickup truck was in danger of repo. He was behind on his mortgage.

He was leaning over the abyss, waiting for a downdraft.

Mitch blew out his brains on Tuesday with a pistol he'd bought from Jerry his best friend and head of L's frame shop. The workshop got the news at 3. After six month's on disability, Mitch had come back to work. He'd work two days a week, never calling when he stayed home, pushing L to enough. L was carrying his medical insurance. He went by the book: issued warnings, conferred with the Union, mailed last chance agreements, and finally he canceled Mitch's insurance by mail.

Wednesday morning Jerry calls on 0774 and I answer. Momentary stunned silence, then normal as can be: "Oh, hi Paul, I'm looking for L or Sam." I walk down the hall and tell Sam to pick up. Before I can hang up I hear Jerry scream to Sam that we're all lucky he's seeing his psychiatrist this afternoon or he might come down and kill us. He slams down the phone. L calls the police at my suggestion and tells the two officers who come that Jerry has guns. They leave for Jerry's house to disarm him.

An hour later Jerry rushes past my office, shouting that he wants his pay (L tells me later he was about to put it in the mail). I look up from my keyboard as Jerry passes. I see no weapon and I continue writing out a price list.

Jerry shouts at L: "You didn't pull the trigger but you killed him. My appointment with my psychiatrist is all that stands between you and death."

Afterwards, Sam's palms are wet. There are circles of perspiration on his shirt. He keeps repeating: "Man, he said he was gonna shoot us." L is calm. He keeps a Colt semi-automatic in his desk drawer. He'd stepped into the hall during Jerry's tirade, right hand behind his back, and gestured at me with his left hand to get out of the line of fire.

There are ripples of fear among the sewers. The Puerto Rican springers Mitch despised watch L to see what he's going to do. The afternoon is spent changing locks and alarm settings (Jerry as head of the woodshop has keys), making calls to Jerry's psychiatrist who makes a confidentiality disclaimer then asks for word by word details; calling the Union president. Roy, the output manager, says this reminds him of the time he found a corpse in the men's room at Stoddard Chevrolet. Two days later Jerry swears to a Union disciplinary committee that he doesn't remember a thing.

First Union Bank, 7th and Tilghman, 2 in the afternoon, stopping for cash to pay my grunts. My truck is loaded to the gills with furniture I scored at a factory closing. A line at the ATM. A Puerto Rican woman in bulging tights is cursing at it, banging it like it's a pinball machine, taking her card out, putting it back in, not getting the result she wants. Finally she senses the long line behind her and storms off snarling. Just another dole day at the branch they all can walk to. Open late because of a federal fairness clause. The branch gets theirs back by beating the jerks with fees. A person can lose half their pay in thirty-five dollar bounced check fees. Inside, long lines of Blacks and Ricans. Long delays as customers argue with tellers. The tellers explain, speaking slowly like to children, that the funds won't be available for four days. Aunts, fathers, boyfriends, wait beside the arguer hoping for a sliver of dole.

At 4, on Lumber Street, unloading onto my warehouse dock. It's 93, has begun to rain lightly. Andy, Bill and Romeo are soaked with sweat. A little hoodlum, maybe 8 or 9, gallops across the dirty wet alley.

What ya doin?

Unloading furniture from an auction.

He's 5' 2", no shirt, no shoes, dripping socks, a dirty blond buzzcut. He nods appraisingly, rubs his chin, introduces himself.

I'm Matthew.

I'm Paul.

We smile at each other and nod.

Matthew grunts with my guys as they wield a conference table.

That's big stuff. Where'd you get that stuff?

I told you. At an auction. Where are your shoes?

In my bedroom. Mom's in there. Oh, don't drop it, don't drop it! Ha!

Does she know you're out here?

Nah.

She doesn't care?

Nope.

Where's your father?

Mom threw him out last week. The cops came. He doesn't pay his bills. They're coming back for me.

Yeh? Why is that?

Because I smoke cigarettes and drink coffee, yep.

Where do you get the cigarettes?

The baby-sitter gives them to me. She lives down the block. She lets me smoke for not telling Mom that she goes home as soon as Mom leaves.

How many do you smoke at a time?

Five.

He dances across the alley.

Come 'ere, Paul. He points at an oil slick. Look. A rainbow.

VICTORIA FRANZESE

A New York City Mom

TUESDAY, APRIL 29, 2008
Baseball

So, a friend wondered in a recent email, how is baseball season going? So far it is going great. My younger son's team has 3 coaches (plus Darling Husband and I who share the "bench coach" role). While the coaches lamented recently that we're 0 for 2 regarding weekly snacks, we are 2 for 2 game-wise, so that's ok.

At least I think we won the last game. I was too busy keeping little leaguers in the dugout, keeping track of the batting order, providing Kleenexes and water bottles, etc. to be absolutely sure. But I shouldn't worry too much about not focusing on watching the game itself: I will have plenty of time in future games to keep track of the score because apparently I embarrassed my son by insisting that the kids cheer on their teammates and so he doesn't want me to oversee the bench anymore. Again and again he's told me in the days since (with overtones of The Donald): "You're fired!"

It could be worse. Last year my older son banned me from his games for a while because once, when his team was losing and showing a dispirited lack of pep, I told them to "show a little hustle" as they walked from the field to the dugout. I can now go to games again, but I'm not sure he's forgiven me.

THURSDAY, MAY 1, 2008
Pop-Tarts (based on the beginning of Allen Ginsberg's "Howl")

I saw the best food in the kitchen destroyed by junk, fattening

sugary delicious,
transforming itself from wholesomeness for those who rummage
    through the cabinets looking for a sweet fix,
bright-colored concoctions aching for the primeval connection to the
    hungry palate as the sky gets light in the morning,
which affluence and abundance and tempting and luscious sat there waiting in its
    silver foil with the outline of cartoon figures floating across the top
    contemplating popular kid-culture,
which bared its body to the toaster, between red-heated coils and felt heavenly warmth
    melting the insides and crisping the outsides,
which passed through test kitchens and focus groups with radiant packaging for trendsetting mall-
    rife America and the denizens of the elementary schools,
which was expelled from the city restaurants for too many transfats & oozing candy sprinkles
    from the icing-covered surface of the crust,
which tempts, calls out to us, alluring in strawberry or chocolate-flavored coating and
    hiding soft gooey tastiness inside, good to eat a thousand years.

TUESDAY, FEBRUARY 3, 2009
Maybe Abu is Right After All

My kids love *The Simpsons*, which makes fairly consistent references to the Hindu concept of reincarnation, and *House*, in which Dr. Gregory House insists that there is no afterlife at all—that life on earth is all there is. DH and I are raising the kids Lutheran, with the classic concept of heaven as a reward for a life well lived. Of course, I hope it will be decades until they find out what really happens after you die, but meanwhile, David Eagleman raises some interesting idea about what the afterlife might hold in his book *Sum: Forty Tales From the Afterlives*. He suggests that perhaps we'll be able to look back on scenes from our lives, watching the maple tree you planted as it grows, and your loved ones as they age. Another possibility, is that we'll be able to live our lives over again, except this time life is scrambled so that all time brushing teeth is done consecutively, all time looking for keys is done together, etc. The ultimate message is, of course, that if you live in the present, and enjoy and appreciate the gift of each moment, it doesn't really matter as much what the afterlife holds for us.

WEDNESDAY, MARCH 25, 2009
Dressing for the Weather

These last weeks have been all topsy-turvy weather-wise in NYC, with 60 degree temperatures one day, followed by a surprise snow storm just a few days later. It has been a struggle to get the kids to dress appropriately: their hearts scream "spring" even as the thermometer reads below freezing, and so they insist on sweatshirts as outwear while I try to cajole them into their ski jackets.

The first time I encountered this conflict, my older son was a toddler, probably about three or so, and was insistent on having his way with everything. I've always been a "pick your battles" kind of mom—so many things don't really matter in the long run—and after days of forcing him to wear a heavy coat which he insisted was too hot, allowed him to walk home from daycare without it. I figured that if he got cold he'd just ask for it, and that would be that.

As it turns out, there are apparently plenty of folks who truly believe that "it takes a village" to raise a child and that they have a responsibility to impose their version of proper parenting on anyone they encounter. Several blocks from home, an older woman fell in step next to us and began berating me. I couldn't possibly be my son's mother, she insisted, because no good mother would allow her child to be outdoors on a cold day without a winter coat. My assertion that he didn't want to wear it fell on deaf ears, and she continued to follow us for about five or six blocks, bad-mouthing my parenting skills all the way.

TUESDAY, APRIL 7, 2009
I Love NY!

Former NYC mayor Ed Koch once said, "New York is not a problem. New York is a stroke of genius!" That's pretty much how I feel. Now that he is approaching his golden years, he's purchased a burial plot in Manhattan, so he'll never have to live elsewhere. Hooray for him!

I remember at a work function years ago talking with a group of colleagues about where we would live if money were no object and we could choose to live anywhere in the world. I had just come back from the paradise known as Hawaii, and so folks were surprised to hear that I'd stay right here in NY. But I would. I really love it here.

THURSDAY, MAY 28, 2009
How about a Hug?

My younger son got in trouble at school recently for exuberantly expressing his feeling for a friend with a chest bump. His school has a policy of zero tolerance for physical contact between students—and so the boys were suspended from recess for three days (the exact same punishment as a girl who punched another child in the nose so hard it bled).

I thought about this policy as I read today's *NY Times* article about the new trend among teenagers for saying hello with a hug. Many of the adults interviewed for the article expressed concern about this practice—indeed, several schools have banned hugs altogether. So whatever happened to "hugs not drugs"? Do we really distrust kids and teens that much that we must forbid innocent expressions of affection? Truly, I think the experts have it wrong on this one...

MONDAY, APRIL 5, 2010
April Fools Day

The kids were off from school last week and so the first day of April was a marathon of pranks and practical jokes. I have to admit I started the whole thing by telling the boys that I had just heard on the radio that two days of vacation had been cancelled to make up for the two snow days they had enjoyed a month earlier. They bought it for a moment—and so were determined to "get" me back.

Their first attempt at payback was to spike my half-and-half with vinegar. Luckily, I spotted the bottle on the kitchen counter and knew something was up before I put it into my coffee (serves them right for not putting stuff away!!).

They were more successful a bit later, though. While I was out for a run, they vaselined the door handle of my office and completely wrapped my office chair and phone in saranwrap. Just for good measure, they added a whoopee cushion to the seat of my chair.

I thought they were done, but they still had a few tricks up their sleeves. While I showered, they emptied all the shelves in my closet, hiding all my pants and tops in my husband's armoire (they hid his clothes somewhere else). Thankfully, I had just done laundry and so found some clean clothes to wear even before I discovered where they had put all my clothes.

Hubby didn't get off without being pranked, either. In addition to moving his clothes around, they saran-wrapped his desk chair and phone, too, adding a "ha, ha!" message written in shaving cream as an extra creative touch.

What a fun day!

MONDAY, APRIL 19, 2010
Gymnastics in the Subway

I've been riding the NYC subway for 24 years and thought I had seen the full range of underground performers (even before the fabulous *Music Under New York* program kicked in). Back in the late 80's, there was an amazing violinist who played with enough passion and verve that he had enthusiastic listeners who stopped to applaud even in the midst of the madness in Grand Central Station at rush hour. I've seen plenty of other musicians, too—everything from Julliard students who want to earn a few extra dollars while they practice, to men on steel drums, groups with Andean flutes, jazz ensembles, old timers with accordions... the list goes on and on. I've seen singers in all shapes, sizes and talent levels: well-rehearsed a capella groups, vocalists with mikes and synthesizers (and CDs for sale), and plenty of beggars who literally sing for their supper (*Amazing Grace* is always a favorite with the latter). I'm old enough that I even remember the preponderance of break dancers (what fun!) in the early and mid-80's. Jugglers? Yup, seen plenty of those, too. But until recently, I had never seen a group of guys perform an amazing gymnastics routine in a moving subway car. I was absolutely astounded at the work and diligent practice that must have gone into perfecting their act—so much so that I gave them a $20 bill for their efforts—something that I never do. Want to be astounded yourself? Check them out on YouTube.

THURSDAY, MAY 20, 2010
The Easy Way Out

An assignment to
Cross off the list.
Rather relax; why do I have to waste time
On homework, he asks.
Silly me, I say,
To think that writing a poem could be meaningful!
It's not; it's
Crap, I'm told.

Possibly the worst assignment ever!
OMG - I can't believe my teacher is making me do this!
Ever more and
More complaints.. then.. in two seconds he writes a
Simple acrostic poem. Done!

FRIDAY, MAY 28, 2010
Doing Your Best

I've started to read *Nurture Shock: New Thinking About Children* by Po Bronson and Ashley Merryman, which, among other things, describes the need to praise kids for their actions and efforts rather than their innate talents and intelligence. The thinking is that rewarding kids for getting A's by telling them that they are smart eventually backfires when the kids inevitably run across something that is difficult for them: they think that if they were really smart, they'd be able to answer the question easily; and when they don't know the answer right away, they think it's because they aren't smart after all (rather than because problem-solving takes effort). I'm not sure that I buy into this line of thinking. I believe that some people really are smart and it is ok to recognize that. Of course, anything worth achieving does take effort, so the message that you should always work hard is a good one, too. But I'm not convinced that the two are mutually exclusive.

In any event, I was thinking of the value of always doing your best when I read *The Tipsy Diaries* column in today's *New York Times*. The piece describes Doug Quinn, the bartender extraordinaire at the legendary P. J. Clarke's. He went to college (Vassar even) but here he is making the humble task of bartending his life's work. *The Times* alludes to the position as lucrative (even just in tips, he probably pulls in upwards of $1000 a night), but more than anything, the paper makes it clear that Quinn has taken his God-given talents of "speed, stamina, dexterity, personality and an awe-inspiring memory" and worked them to the point that he is clearly acknowledged as one of the best in his profession.

THURSDAY, AUGUST 4, 2011
My Boy's Grown Up

Everyone remarks about how mature and tall my 13-year old son has become. And he is. He's 5' 11" and likely to add even more inches in the next few years. As he's grown taller, he has also slimmed down, and his face has lost its roundness and become manlier.

But to me, one of the most surprising changes has been the change in his voice. He didn't undergo any sort of awkward transformation, but rather seemed to change overnight. I hadn't noticed it until one day I got out of the shower and heard a man in my apartment. It was in the middle of the afternoon (I had just come back from a run)—I knew my husband was at work and couldn't imagine who it was. The doorman hadn't buzzed me. What was going on??!! What a shock to discover that the deep voice belonged to my son!!

And then just like that, I got used to it, so that when I subsequently left a voicemail on his cellphone, I was surprised to hear the old little-boy voice that he had used to set up the voice-mailbox. And on his confirmation day at church, people remarked about his deep, deep voice, and I was surprised that they were surprised.

WEDNESDAY, AUGUST 10, 2011
Lying to Your Kids

I recently read an article about the lies we tell our kids that makes lying seem ok, and even, well, fun. I struggle with this view of the world. Lying to get kids to wear seatbelts in the car or to stop kicking the seat on an airplane? I understand being harried and quickly coming up with these falsehoods in a moment of weakness, but I hope these parents followed up at some point and told their kids the truth. And telling kids that ice cream is really cauliflower so that they won't want any seems to me to just avoiding the difficulty of saying "you can't have ice cream right now"—and I find that a symptom of the perennial problem of parents who can't say "no."

There is no doubt that it is difficult to tell the truth sometimes. Kids ask tough questions at times when you're not expecting them. When my son was about 2 or 3 he asked where babies come from in a crowded elevator—and you've never seen an elevator empty out so fast! More recently, my boys have expressed curiosity about our finances and income—and the temptation to coat the truth is certainly there. But instead, DH and I tell them that we don't want to discuss it with them at this point, that we don't think the numbers are meaningful until they can really understand the larger context.

I remember when I was little, my mom referred to beer as my dad's "brown medicine" (because his brand came in brown bottles). I still don't know why she did that. Why not just say "it's beer and it's not for kids?"

SUNDAY, SEPTEMBER 11, 2011
Remembering September 11th

I tried to ignore the anniversary activities for the most part this weekend. Mostly, I just remembered what that day was like. The sky was so blue. Life seemed so full of possibilities: not just the usual back-to-school feelings that every September brings, but so much more.

I had just dropped my kids off at daycare/pre-school when I heard that a plane had hit one of the towers. Like many others, I imagined a small craft, like the plane that hit the Empire State Building. I was surprised when another mother worried about her husband's trip to a medical convention in Europe; it seemed inconceivable that a little accident would affect the busy NYC airports.

My own husband was also traveling—I knew that he was flying back from Texas after an overnight trip, but I expected that he'd go straight to the office and I wouldn't see him until evening. As it turns out, his flight never got off the ground. When he got off the plane and out of the airport, he went straight to the mall to pick up some extra underwear, socks and such, since he didn't know how long it would be before he made it home. It turned out to be almost a week.

He called, as I returned home and encouraged me to turn on the TV. What I saw was horrifying. The fridge and pantry were well stocked, but he encouraged me to pick up a few more things at the grocery store just in case. I also picked up some cash—with the nation under attack, who knew what was going to happen? We talked about me driving the kids to our weekend house in PA if things in the city got worse (but ultimately this was a moot point -- no one was going anywhere in or out of Manhattan).

I hurriedly collected my kids from school/daycare. I needed them with me—just in case. The facility is associated with Mt. Sinai and I volunteered to pick up any other kids whose parents were needed at the hospital—at this point we all thought there would be lots of casualties and that the NYC medical facilities would be overwhelmed with the wounded. Of course that didn't happen, and as the hours and hours of TV watching that day (and the next) wore on, an ongoing clip was of the staff at St. Vincent's Hospital as they waited for patients.

I watched TV non-stop for 2 days. Amazingly, my boys (then 4 years old and 5 months old) hung out quietly as I watched the towers fall again and again. At one point we ventured out briefly and discovered that the odd smell that had pervaded our neighborhood was actually from the smoldering World Trade Center. I had seen wisps of smoke in the distance, but wasn't prepared for that acrid smell.

The loss of the firefighters hit me the hardest. They had been heroes to our boys. They represented everything strong and manly, pure and true. My older son dressed up as a firefighter for Halloween and we had made many trips to the Fire Zone together. So when the plea went out for donations of socks for the rescue crews, we happily complied. I think we donated food, too. Like many other kids, my son drew pictures of the images he had seen. It seemed to have affected him deeply, at least at the time.

My younger son remembers nothing of course. He was just too little. But every time I write the 2001 of his birth date, I think of that day.

SUNDAY, JUNE 21, 2015
The Greatest Gift My Father Ever Gave Me

Before my high school graduation, the officials in charge of the ceremony made it clear to the graduating seniors that we were to walk in and out in two straight lines and that we were not to throw our caps into the air. They were very vehement about wanting to maintain an air of decorum throughout all of the proceedings. As Salutatorian, I walked at the head of the class next to my friend Christa, who was Valedictorian. We followed the rules as we processed in, during our speeches (we both addressed the class), and throughout the distribution of the diplomas. But halfway through the march out, we could contain our exuberance no longer. With great joy befitting the culmination of the years of hard work and studying, we tore off our mortarboards and tossed them into the air, and breaking ranks, we sprinted to the exit.

The local newspaper ran a headline about the "bedlam" that had ensued, although the article was clearly sympathetic to our youthful high spirits. But the school administrators were apoplectic. In subsequent years, graduates received fake diplomas during the ceremony that could only be exchanged for the real thing if the class behaved well. And my father, who owned the small printing business that had printed school materials for decades, no longer received orders from the school district, as punishment for siring such a "troublemaker."

Despite the impact on his finances, my dad proudly told everyone he knew about the incident, proclaiming with glee that his daughter has "spunk." His delight in rearing a strong, rules-be-damned woman was truly the greatest gift he could ever give me. At a time when many girls were taught to be quiet and demure, he encouraged me to be bold, demonstrative and courageous. I'll always be grateful.

JUDITH FARMER MILLER

Everybody Has Their Song

My father, William Farberman, was born into a musical family in Williamsburg, Brooklyn in 1905. He was the youngest of four children. His father was a professional musician and his mother was a homemaker.

When he was thirteen years old, Willie got his first job as a drummer with the Carl Fenton Orchestra. At the time, he was playing violin but the band needed a drummer. His brother, who was already playing with the Fenton Orchestra, insisted Willie was a drummer and should be given the job. It was true, in any case, that Willie had by this time made himself into a pretty good percussionist—so his brother's story wasn't a complete fabrication.

Willie went on to play and record with many of the big bands, including Glen Gray and the Casa Loma Band, Red Nichols, Tommy Dorsey and Charlie Spivack.

In 1932 while playing in the Larry Siry Band at the Simplon Club, a Prohibition era Speakeasy in Manhattan, the *maitre de* fired the bandleader because he was a drunk, and my father's career as an orchestra leader began.

Not long afterwards, Dad gave himself a stage name and formed his own group, Willie Farmer and the Farmer in the Dell Orchestra. Part of the Big Band phenomenon of the 30s, they thrived throughout The Great Depression. The Farmer in the Dell Orchestra toured extensively throughout the East and Midwest. They played regularly at "Cafe Society" dinner clubs in Manhattan, such as El Morocco, the Promenade Café, the Rainbow Room in Rockefeller Center, Radio City, Coconut Grove atop the Park Central Hotel, and The Tavern on the Green.

The band also performed for many early radio broadcasts. They were heard on the National Broadcasting System's WEAF-WJZ and Mutual Broadcasting System's WOR. Willie's more than forty recordings for Victor and Bluebird are considered collectibles among vinyl aficionados. In addition, the band played at many private parties for celebrities including Cole Porter and Robert Wagner. They performed for the Grand Council College graduation with the Archbishop of New York, Francis Cardinal Spellman, presiding; and for Mike Todd's, *America, Be Seated*, a modern minstrel show at the 1964 World's Fair.

The band broke up during World War II. Thereafter my father did club dates and played at private parties and dances in the New York area and later Florida where he and my mother moved in 1972. He died on April 5,1990 at eighty-four. His musical career lasted sixty-five years.

When I was growing up I resented the fact that my father worked weekends. While other kids' Dads were regularly home at night, mine never was. I was five years old when I first heard his band at the Promenade Cafe at Rockefeller Center. It left such an impression on me that I still remember what I ate for lunch that day. The next time I heard him play was at a friend's wedding in the 1950s. I had always thought Dad despised being a musician, but seeing him on stage it was obvious that he was having a delightful time. When I confronted him about this, his response was: "I love people having a good time because of my music. It's the business I hate!"

He was a very handsome and charming man, meticulously groomed in his custom tailored tuxedo. He turned the heads of many women who came to his gigs. His charm, however, was not only in his looks but in his heart and his affection for the people for whom he performed. He was genuinely interested in his audiences and always played what they wanted to hear.

After he died, I found a list he'd put together of songs, each of which he associated with particular film stars and New York City movers and shakers. I don't know if the tunes were these peoples' favorites or not, but the list shows how much delight Willie took in indulging his idea that everybody has their song. Here are a few:

William Farmer and His Farmer in the Dell Orchestra
"Farmer in the Dell"

Duchess of Argyle
"No Fool like An Old Fool"

Don Ameche
"Silk Stockings"
"Diane"

Lee Bowman
"Too Beautiful For Words"

D. Biddle
"Just a Gigalo"
"Falling in Love Again"
"Silk Stockings"

Jack Benney
"Love In Bloom"

Bob Considine
"The Very Thought Of You"

And Mrs. Bob (Millie) Considine
"Noholata Tuxedo Junction"
"Sound Of Music"

Hoagy Carmichael
"One Morning in May"
"Ole Buttermilk Sky"

Truman Capote
"A Sleeping Bee"

Betty Davis
"They're Either Too Young or Too Old"
"The Best is yet to Come"

Frank Farrell
"I Remember April"
"Fly Me to the Moon"

Mrs. Henry Ford
"More"

Ann Ford
"Start of Something Big"

Red Buttons
"More"

Mr. Henry Ford
"Paper Moon"
"True to You in My Fashion"
"More"

Charley Farrell
"Charley My Boy"
"I'm A Dreamer"

Za Za Gabor
"Where Is Your Heart"

Madga Gabor
"Getting To Know You"

Kathy/Suzy Seche
"Wait Till You See Her"
"Clear Day"
"Best Is Yet To Come"

Hermoine Gingold
"Milk & Honey"

Mr. Hershfield & Girlfriend
"Foolish Heart"
"More"

"Fly Me to the Moon"

Frank Hunter Club 21 Brass
"Funny Valentine"
"Change My Plans"

Senator Halpern
"I Could Write a Book"

Hope Hampton
"Most Beautiful Girl in the World"

Bob Hope
"Thanks for the Memory"

George Hamilton
"You're All the World to Me"

Sonja Henie
"Honey"

Young Javitz & Wife
"Too Young"

Kybar Kahn
"Goody Goody"

Princess of Monaco (Grace Kelly)
"True Love"

Mrs. McLean
"Married I Can Always Get"
"From This Moment On"

Contess Maruscha (Announcer Don Wilson's Former Wife)
"La Vie En Rose"

Mr. Louis Marx (Toy Maker)
"As Time Goes By"

Connie Constance Moore
"Stella by Starlight"

Hal Roach Jr.
"People Will Say"

Society Columnist Nancy Randolph
"Sweetest Sounds"

Mrs. Winthrop Rockefeller (Former Jeanette Edris)
"Dancing On the Ceiling"

Toots Shor
"Toot Toot Tootsie GoodBye"

Lou Sobels
He: "Meloncholy Baby"
She: "Peg of My Heart"

Mr. Speilman from Speilman Chevrolet Motors (Brooklyn)
"San Francisco"
"Chicago"
"My Kind of Town"

G. B. MILLER

Director's Notes

SAILOR'S HAT

I staggered up from my seat in the bar, swinging wildly, and knocked the daylights out of one Robert Lomax. It was the role in theatre that I had waited for...

The production was *The World of Suzie Wong* at the original Hunterdon Hills Playhouse, and it was my first time working as an Equity apprentice, on an Equity production, in an Equity house.

The responsibilities of an apprentice encompass all things theatre. An apprentice is expected to clean the stage, operate sound systems, paint sets, build props, and—most importantly—to observe.

I was a young actor with big dreams, willing to do anything in theatre to get my Equity card, the magical passport to working in legit theatre.

Finally, I got my big chance. I was given a walk-on role in ...*Suzie Wong*, right aside the professionals. It was only a few moments onstage, but I rehearsed it intensely, and felt proud and confident of my work.

Cut to Opening night, Friday, June 13, 1962.

On cue, I stumbled onstage, sat down in the bar, took off my sailor's hat, flung it down on a table, and waited for my cue to stroll up to leading man Craig Stevens (of Peter Gunn fame), start a drunken brawl, punch him out, and exit stage left.

End of scene. Lights to black. Whew! I'd been brilliant in the role, if I did say so myself!

A moment later, lights come up on the next scene. As I stood in the wings gloating over my talents, I noticed that my sailor's hat was still on the bar table, forgotten. Oh no! I had to remedy my mistake, and fast. So I casually strolled out onstage, sat down at the table, put on my hat, and strolled off. As I walked off stage, the audience exploded with laughter and applauded madly.

Suddenly, the stage manager pulled me back into the wings—and fired me on the spot. It seems that a period of oh, five years had passed between my big fight scene, and the scene I had just sauntered into to retrieve my forgotten hat.

Today, when I direct hungry young actors, so eager for perfection, I encourage them to explore, and to stumble, knowing that their mistakes will teach them everything they really need to know.

FROM THE ARTISTIC DIRECTOR

Over The River And Through The Woods—a vivid memory......of my imagination.

Since I was a child, I'd always wanted to live in a stone farmhouse in the country, and raise a nanny goat which I would name Jeff Davis.

After almost 70 years, my dream came true when Kate and I moved into "the stone manor house down the lane, over the Jordan Creek, and through the woods." After having lived in Ireland, yet another dream had come true... this was to be the best of all Christmases—"as white as Lapland."

This 1794 Troxell farmhouse stands on the land of pioneering men and women who left behind memories of their own childhoods. We named our new home Anam Cara Farm—Anam Cara being the Irish for "soul teacher" (and the title of a beloved book by the Irish spiritual writer and poet John O'Donohue)—so that we may share our artistic dreaming with others.

What better a place to invite our friends—a gentle place, white with snows, a warm fireplace, glittering lights, a welcoming journey over the Jordan and through the black walnuts and ash trees.....to hear the words of Dylan Thomas as he recollected his own childhood and youth in Wales.

Now, anyone know where I can adopt a nanny goat ?

(A Child's Christmas in Wales, December 2013 @ Anam Cara)

SLIDES

1. Before I could recall the lines of the play, nearing the end of the second act, I came close to true fear and panic; a fellow actor

caught my plummet and re-phrased the thought. Saved again.

2.   On stage we had a broken chair which always tumbled when you sat it on it: my turn came, the audience wept, and I would fall with dignity knowing it would happen again.

3.   I can still hear my father's voice as he taught me to project on stage; he would shout in angry tones—"you never do anything right," and "you'll never be an actor." After a lifetime, he can't stop that same speech although he is somewhere else now and I hear him coming from all directions.

4.   I don't know why I would be directing a show if it wasn't for giving some sort of voice to people who are out on the edge of life itself.

5.   "You know the first scene in the second act isn't working. Work on that with more passion. Audiences aren't stupid…anymore." Did I say that?

6.   It was the nude scene in "The Assassination and Prosecution of Jean Paul Marat as Performed by the Inmates of the Asylum of Charenton under the Direction of the Marquis DeSade." In the healing tub most of the play, I stood up, the towel fell on cue, and I could hear the gasps from the audience. What reaction did I expect!? Why were they so surprised?

7.   The magic on stage begins when one single voice from the audience reassures me that they are listening.

8.   What I am looking for in a script is whether the play excites me to think, touches me, or just haunts me. It's a "feeling" more than anything else. I've learned to trust that.

9.   The Scene: A morning. Summery sun. Lights come up, warmth, then waves of heat. A tingling sensation in the fingers. A hesitation. You hear the clearing of the throat, then the crinkle of candy wrappers - and you know you are fortunate to be an actor on stage.

10.   I was only fired once as a director. I failed to agree with the producer twice and three times I allowed an actor to miss rehearsal. The show doesn't necessarily go on.

TO KILL A MOCKINGBIRD
Director's Notes

" Miss Jean Louise, stand up. Your father's passin'. "

I first read *To Kill a Mockingbird* after I graduated from high school in 1960. I must admit, having grown up in the small anthracite coal town of Tamaqua, I didn't find it that startling—in fact, it felt oddly familiar.

Lee's beautifully-crafted and poignant tale of the ugliness—and of the greatness—inside us all, slipped past my adolescent mind in lieu of college plans, girls, Ford Mustangs and a hated after-school job.

But as I look back, I realize what else was so familiar to me about Mockingbird ... I realize that the people of my hometown had often exhibited kindness I never would have imagined, that they somehow were able to respect each other's differences, and honor each other's journey in life, even my own teenage trials and tribulations. In my heart, I stood up and thanked them for their support and compassion.

Harper Lee's classic is about many things...the Depression and small town life, about race, class, and all the things that divide us, and about coming of age.

Compassionate, dramatic and deeply moving, Mockingbird is also about choosing courage, the courage to do what is right, the outcome notwithstanding. It is about growing up emotionally, no matter what the age. It is about empathy—about learning to walk in another person's shoes before judging them.

To Kill a Mockingbird portrays a society that is often staggeringly unfair; but it suggests that doing something to make life a little more fair for all, even if it seems like it's not having any effect, is still worthwhile, and what's more, admirable.

This timeless play has so much to say to our own angry, divisive times. It's timeless, as powerful today as it was over 50 years ago, and it asks us to bear witness to our own spiritual and ethical beliefs.

So stand up...everyone...stand up. Compassion—and a great soul of a story—are passin'. Embrace it.

G. BRUCE BOYER

Snapshots from the Ward

1. Leroy

I met LeRoy the third time I checked into a hospital ward for chronic depression which started when I was a young adult and sometimes the medications didn't keep me in check, so whichever psychiatrist I was seeing at the time would suggest a little holiday in one of these places. The idea was that the stay would keep you safe from suicide til another drug that worked could be found. I never said no, even though I knew what I was getting myself into. Soul clogging boredom, bad food, being treated like a child by the nurses and staff, being treated like a geriatric idiot by the doctors, and a complete lack of freedom in a particularly threatening way. It was no weekend at the Villa d'Este.

The rec room always had a TV tuned in to the soap operas or even sometimes the shopping network, and there were tons of three-year old magazines around, with the subscription address cut out. Often there were crayons, balls of acrylic yarn, and playing cards.

***

Just once I'd seen a patient come close to killing himself. He'd somehow found a bathroom with a lock on the door—locks are unheard of on these wards, except for the doors that lead outside—locked himself in, smashed the wall mirror with his fist and slit his throat with a shard of the glass. He was, incredibly, still alive when they saw the blood seep out under the door several minutes later and broke the door open.

***

Meds were given with a regularity and inevitability rivaling the medieval practice of ringing the times for prayer by the watchful psychiatric nurses. Unhealthful meals consisting mainly of starch were served by orderlies and taken in a communal dining room. There were daily group therapy sessions and crafts therapy, and every day or so a psychiatrist would conduct a perhaps five-minute interview with each patient. These consisted of a series of innocuous questions: How are you feeling? Have you thought about suicide lately? Have you been eating and going to the group therapy sessions? Have you been getting a good night's sleep? If you expected to eventually leave, you answered the questions correctly. I'm feeling not as jittery and nervous, and I haven't been thinking about suicide lately. I actually like the group sessions, and the food's o.k. I still take the sleeping medication, but I sleep right through the night. It obviously wasn't a good idea to say you were feeling beamingly hopeful at the very beginning. The indifference and the lying had an easy partnership.

The doctor would say he thought you were doing better, and you would tell the next person in the hall to come in on your way out. Otherwise you were pretty much on your own to sit in the communal room and re-read a copy of People, or sleep on your bed in your room, walk the halls of the ward, clockwise, then counter-clockwise, then clockwise again, or just sit in the hall for ten or twelve hours. There was always a public phone or two in a hallway so patients could both make and receive calls. Some got calls and made them all the time, others never. I once noticed a woman constantly watching the shopping network shows, then race to the phone and order everything she saw. She must have memorized her credit card numbers and had the loot sent to her home.

After a while patients usually made a friend or two to talk with and while away the hours. They'd sit next to each other in crafts therapy, at meals, in the hall. Others were withdrawn and isolated within themselves, and whose sorrow was perhaps so inconsolable that they'd crossed over that river of melancholy into an unreachable place. Some faces were a dull blank, others broke out in deep or wailing sobs every few minutes or so, some stared angrily at everyone. Women tended to gravitate to one group, men to another. Or perhaps women consorting with men was discouraged. Or perhaps having difficulties with the opposite sex was the reason some of them were here.

***

I struck up an ongoing conversation with LeRoy, a Black guy in his early thirties from the North Philly ghetto. LeRoy was street-smart, the kind of guy you'd see hanging out in a poolroom, maybe hustling games, maybe other things. He was hip and appeared laid-back, but I knew he had a problem with alcohol and drugs. He wasn't taken in by the false, patronizing camaraderie of the place one bit, but he played the game with finesse and expertise.

For some reason we hit it off. We talked mainly about music, jazz and R&B, and women, which of the nurses might be seduced into our rooms. The philosophy of the incarcerated. We sat with each other at meals, and next to each other at group and never spoke up unless we were called on. We knew you were expected to participate at group; that was one of the staff's touchstones for normalcy. LeRoy and I were quick studies. We were positive and enthusiastic, with just an occasional note of despair for balance and to convey the impression that we needed them. That was always a good note to hit.

Group Director: LeRoy, how do you feel about being here now?

LeRoy: Well, it's given me a chance to think about my problems and I've changed my mind about some things. I see that I've got to take responsibility for my own life more, y'know. The frustration and the depression comes and goes, but I'm working on it.

Group Director: Bruce, would you agree with that?

Me: I think I would. I mean, you can't change other people, y'know. You got to change yourself. I'm beginning to see that. It's attitude that's the most important. I'm starting to understand that.

We were very adept. We never rocked the boat, even though we were perfectly willing to sink the ship. What was the sense in pointing out it was all bullshit? You'd never get out then. Maybe you'd end up someplace worse, like a state facility.

I had quit cigarettes years before, but LeRoy still liked to smoke, so if friends came to visit me I'd ask them to bring along a pack or two for him. He'd reciprocate by giving me his dessert or treating me to a coke. We got on well. One day when we were sitting in the communal room alone, I asked him how he got into this place.

"Oh, man, it was the most fabulous fuckup. Didn't I tell you? The thing is, you know I'm an alcoholic, yeah? Well I was doing some steady drinking and then I added some coke and shit, and it got real serious real fast. My woman left me, I couldn't get no money finally. I even went to a doctor who gave me some pills that were supposed to make you sick if you had a drink. I took the pills and drank anyway, and got so sick I gave up the pills.

"It was a real fuckin' mess, y'know, and I came to the point where I knew I had to kill myself. I couldn't see no other way. So I stole a gun, but I just couldn't do it. I walked out on the Ben Franklin Bridge, but I couldn't jump. It was a bitch, man. I wanted to throw myself off the subway platform, anything, but I couldn't. Such pain, and yet I didn't have the courage, isn't that a bitch? And then I got my great idea, my great plan.

"You know how fast city cops are to shoot someone? Man, you could be standing on the corner holding a Zippo lighter and they'll shoot you 'bout fifty times, right? Happens all the time. So I made my plans. Went down to the hardware store and bought the biggest motherfuckin' ax they had, one of them big heavy ones with a long wood handle.

"Next morning I got up, drank a pint of vodka in my pajamas, grabbed that ax and went out on the stoop. And, man, I started swingin' that ax and yelling how I was gonna kill every motherfucker on the block. I mean it was a scene, baby, and I was tearing it up, yeah, and there was folks running every which way. There was adrenaline flowing on that street like a water main had broke.

"So in about five minutes here they come, three cop cars screech up to the house like some damn gangsta movie. Ya know what those motherfuckers did? They took my ax, beat the living piss outta me, and put me in this shithole. I'm tellin' you, man, you can't trust those fuckin' cops to do nothin' right!"

At the end of the week, during a group session, a nurse came in to tell me I was being discharged. Before I left, I told everybody at the session what a great experience being there had been, and how it had made me think differently about my life, and how I was ready to face the outside world. On the way out, I took LeRoy aside. "I'm gonna miss you, man. You were the only thing in this place that made it seem real. Take care of yourself, y'know?" We shook hands, and he said, "Yeh, you too, Bro. It's a world of trouble."

2. Ruth

In August, on my psychiatrist's suggestion, I'd checked into a hospital that was infatuated with group therapy. It was around the time when shock therapy still hadn't made its comeback, and group sessions were just beginning to be seen as all the rage.

At 11 a.m. every morning between six and ten of us, depending on who felt like showing up, would shuffle into the common room, arrange the chairs into a circle, and a "Director Nurse" would moderate an hourly discussion.

I slept through the hour, unless I was called on to say something, in which case I always said the right thing. "I'm sorry, I'm still having a little trouble following the conversation, but I think some of the points are interesting and giving me a different way of looking at things." I mean, right? No sense in making the director think you weren't appreciating her effort. I've found that psychiatric staff people are almost painfully needy.

One day at the beginning of the week, just as we had arranged our chairs, the director said, "I'd like to introduce a new member of our group. Ruth was just admitted last night, and I think we should all welcome her and introduce ourselves." We all said "Hello, Ruth" as enthusiastically as we could and gave our first names. Ruth, whose head was down and eyes averted, mumbled hello, and we carried on with our discussion, and I returned to nodding and day dreaming.

About three days later and about fifteen minutes into the group session, the director said, "Ruth, you haven't said anything yet since you've been here. Why don't you tell us something about yourself?" I was sipping a cup of weak tea and looking down the hall at the time, just staring off.

"The Lord is angry with me," Ruth said, her head down and face blank.

What? I was only half awake, but it sounded like Ruth had said that the Lord was angry with her.

"Can you tell us why that is?" said the director.

" ...... Because I'm bad," she muttered.

I was awake. What had she done? Shoplifted? Cheated on her income taxes? Cheated on her husband? Killed her children? Voted for a Republican?

There was a long pause. "Why do you think you're bad, Ruth?"

the director said, looking right at her.

Another long pause, a long pause. ......"I've touched myself."

I didn't get it right away. Maybe I was just taking too much Ativan and was missing a lot these days. But the director wasn't as dumb as I thought she was.

"You've masturbated, is that it, Ruth?", she said rather directly.

There was a silence. We were now all looking from Ruth to the director and back again.

"May I ask the group," the director began slowly, " if any of you have ever masturbated?"

Suddenly we were all nodding our heads like chickens and saying how we all masturbated all the time, and how we didn't think there was anything wrong with it. The guy next to me asked me aloud if I masturbated. "Every time I'm not depressed," I said, as loud as I could.

"Ruth," again the director began slowly, "I'd like you to try and think that maybe masturbation's not the sin you think it is. Maybe it's normal."

Ruth's head hadn't moved, and I couldn't tell if there were any anguish, or confusion, or anything in her eyes or not.

"Yeah, normal," we all almost shouted and nodded in unison. And the session ended on that stellar note. My tea had gone cold.

Next morning I was in the common room at 11 sharp and sitting in my chair, watching everyone file in. But Ruth wasn't there.

The director began by asking if anyone had anything they wanted to say. "Yeah," I almost interrupted her, "where's Ruth?"

"She was moved to another ward," the director said abruptly.

Someone started to bitch about the magazines in the common room being 90 years old, and someone else cracked that the hamburgers at lunch were even older. One of the women started in about how her husband and children didn't respect her and started to sob. I sipped my tea and drifted off into a day dream.

3. The Pro

There were several ways to tell which were the patients and which were the doctors on the ward. The shrinks were the ones wearing the nice little white lab coats—names stitched in red on the left chest—

and moving a bit quicker than the patients. Those were the main differences. And that the doctors had an unnerving unemotional stability about them. The patients were both happier and sadder. That always struck me as a great irony, and potentially a great theory: that the experts dealing with the prime mover in motivation were themselves so unemotional. When you're sitting in the hall for fourteen hours a day, you come up with great theories like that.

The nursing staff was a bit less gray, but took all their cues from the doctors and had been steeped in the rules of the game beyond questioning. Their mode was cheerfulness at all costs. There was always the toothy, understanding smile and the soft pat on the shoulder. What else would you do when there was nothing else to do?

So it was the patients who were really the most interesting. But there was one bright spot in the professional heavens. The exception to all the grayness was Dr. Arnold Sheiskopt, a star by any measure. On my very first interview with him—the screening interview that every patient underwent—I was struck strongly with the thought that he would someday have his own TV show. For all I know he may well have now. He had that sort of aura, that sort of energy and elan.

When I met Scheiskopt he had been perfecting his role for probably about a dozen years or so, and he pretty well had it down. While the other doctors were mundanely-but-uniformly dressed in dull suits or even duller casual gear and well-groomed, Sheiskopt was slyly but purposefully disheveled. You know, the slightly baggy trousers and loose-fitting sports jacket (never a suit), the tie slightly askew, the loafers slightly scuffed, the hair just long enough to fall nonchalantly over part of the forehead. The odd button or two left undone. He understood that pose of studied nonchalance, that perfected sense of nor caring that bespoke a higher interest.

He nicely counterbalanced his purposefully disarranged appearance with extreme erudition. Like any good scientist who wanted to be thought genius quality, or in fact like anyone who knows that the true sportsman always plays to opposites, he couched his diagnoses and treatment advice in literary language, interspersing poetic metaphor with quotes from Shakespeare and Churchill, occasionally folk or Black Gospel music and holy scripture. And of course, unlike the other shrinks who flat-lined their emotional responses to other humans, Scheiskopt preferred to heighten his:

bursts of laughter or head-shaking sadness let us know that he really did empathize, that he really did care. Most people—I mean the patients and the staff—found this refreshing and hopeful. Amidst all the hopeless bullshit, there was real bullshit! In the sense that he at least seemed REAL. It reminded me of the old actor's joke: sincerity is what people want, and if you can fake that, you'll be successful.

He was a star. He did interviews with local newspaper, TV, and radio reporters. He was a guest speaker every other week at some convention or other, and not just medical conventions, but civic groups, historical societies, law enforcement confabs, college events. He was a "symposium" sort of guy.

Perhaps the best trick in his bag was his ability to disarm the patient by not only agreeing with him—rather like the priest agreeing with the confessed that the sins of the flesh are strong indeed—but by revealing his own desires. It's a trick I was completely familiar with because writers often use this technique when interviewing someone. It's a way of prying secrets out of them without making a direct assault: I'll confess something, then you confess something. The old quid pro quo approach to the psyche. It's a device that says we're all in it together, aren't we? And in this case, just because you're incarcerated and I'm the warden shouldn't hinder us from having a nice intimate chat, should it?

The first time he used this little device I was, I do confess here, a little taken back by his shamelessness. But this technique was incredibly effective, and why shouldn't he give it a try I thought. Norman Mailer had said somewhere that in psychiatry the patient is not so much changed as aged, and his neuroses exhaust themselves against the analyst's non-responsive reactions. The patient is not so much altered as worn down. Scheiskopf brilliantly took the opposite approach, as all good gamesmen do: his weapon was this role of sincerity. On the ward, he had this part virtually to himself. No one else could come near him for talent and sheer bravado.

At the first mano-a-mano session I had with him, we immediately plunged into the guilt ramifications of wanting to have sex with someone other than your spouse. "Oh," he uttered nonchalantly, "we all do that. I fantasize about that, even of having sex with some of my patients. I know some of my patients fantasize about having sex with me. But of course I understand the psychic damage it would do." I wasn't indelicate enough to ask him, to whom? I didn't want to spoil the moment when he thought he was disarming me.

His confidence grew with succeeding interviews because I offered no resistance. His approach both standard practice and classic to his technique. What was I interested in? I thought he could barely contain himself when I told him I was a literature professor. Did I know the battle horation in Shakespeare's "Henry V"? He not only knew it, he recited it, used it as a wonderful mini lesson on how we must persevere, not lose hope, that we could conquer our depression. It was actually rather brilliant, and I'm sure he thought I well might be his star patient. That I would appreciate him fully, give him his true due. Even the other shrinks didn't really get most of his allusions, but it occurred to him that I would. A patient who would grasp his intellect on a higher level.

4. Muriel

By the time of my latest holiday, shock therapy had once again become the rage. The psychiatrist I found myself with specialized in this procedure and another operation where they implanted a device in your chest that stimulated a nerve that went to your brain and made you feel, apparently, like you didn't have a problem in the world.

But the ward functioned exactly the same as wards I'd been in thirty years before. The same boredom and bad food, the same nurses and the same party line, the same five-minute consultations with the doctors. The only slightly new wrinkle was that, since the invention of the cheap disposable razor, if you wanted to shave, a nurse gave you the razor and stood with you so you wouldn't get any ideas. My first thought was, if you were desperate enough, maybe you'd just kill the nurse first. I decided it was easier to simply not shave.

There was one other interesting thing I noticed after a while. There were no visible wires hanging from the TV or other electrical appliances. I asked a staffer about this and he said that, since this was a newly built hospital, the rooms in this ward were designed without any need for exposed wires, cords, or anything else you could kill yourself with. He said that some patients even used to take the beds apart and use the springs to hang themselves. So now the beds were built without springs. I found this impressive all around. At least someone was thinking in a practical way.

I spent the first couple of days in my room sleeping, but when I did venture out I saw the patients were pretty much the same as usually inhabit the wards: the same teenagers who were surly and confused or naïve and kind of sweet; the same housewives who had tried suicide a half-dozen times; the same alcoholic middle-aged men who'd lost their jobs; some who'd been addicted to prescribed drugs for so long how could you begin to figure out what had been originally wrong? This time, though, there were two new people.

One was a Hell's Angels-style motorcycle guy, complete with the leather jerkin, engineer boots, tattoos, missing teeth, and long, greasy hair. Occasionally he had friends come to visit, guys who looked exactly the same except for their physical build. Motorcycle guys come in all shapes and sizes too. He might have been interesting to talk with, but I was too depressed to try at the beginning, and by the time I could have made the effort, he'd been discharged.

The other person was a woman in her late fifties named Muriel. About 5'4" and weighing about 90 lbs, with no makeup and mousey-colored hair pulled straight back, she looked like a librarian in a concentration camp. Everything about her looked dull. Her clothes were dull and seemed sludge-colored; her face never seemed to show any emotion; she never said anything to anybody, and moved around the halls invisibly. If you saw her at all, walking along, you thought that maybe she walked so delicately because she was brittle and afraid of breaking her bones. Occasionally we found ourselves sitting next to each other on the several groups of chairs lining the hallways. Our eyes never even met. We could have been on different continents.

One late afternoon I was eating some Graham crackers, and she was sitting next to me and so I almost unconsciously offered her one. It took her about an hour-and-a-half to decide, but she finally took it. I'm usually very good with the casual thing, so I didn't show my surprise. A little later she got up and tip-toed away.

A couple of days later the same situation, but this time before she could slide away I said, "My name's Bruce."

"My name is Muriel," she said in a very low, soft way. Not a whisper. It seemed more like a combination of shyness and fear. Or like a lot of decisions were always made on her behalf, but never with her input. She looked like she did what she was told, with no reaction or complaint.

It took another three days to get her to tell me her story. She'd been a research assistant to a science prof at a big university in New England, actually been with this same guy as his assistant for about fifteen years. And then they laid her off, and she was 52 and couldn't get a new job because those sorts of jobs were in short supply and we were going through a bit of a recession anyway and there was nothing. So she spiraled down, had a number of illnesses and no health insurance and within a year and a half all her money was gone and she was in a depression deeper than a snake in the Grand Canyon. And here she was.

"What'll you do when they let you out of here," I asked.

"No idea. No money, no home, no job." And of course her health was iffy and she wasn't young. She was the kind of person that news commentators said "slipped through the cracks," after they're found frozen to death somewhere. But she hadn't slipped through the cracks, she tumbled into a fuckin' dungeon of indifference.

Just two days after that I got the word I'd be discharged the next day. I was more tired of being incarcerated than I was depressed, so I started to tell the psychiatrists what they liked to hear, and got my walking note and prescriptions.

The next day I had to wait 'til 11 in the morning when the doctors came on the ward to get my discharge. I sat down in the hall next to Muriel. I couldn't think of anything to say to her, so I just told her I was leaving in about an hour.

"I wish you could take me with you," she murmured. She meant it more than anything I've ever heard anyone say. I felt sick, and an hour later I left with my prescriptions for anti-depressants.

MARY FLOOD

Road Warrior

I am Home in One Piece

Yesterday was an absolutely gorgeous day which found me running errands from Bolton to Wethersfield to West Hartford. I was cruising along I-384 heading into Hartford thinking that everyone on the road seemed to be feeling pretty mellow and in awe of the beautiful fall day when it happened. Traveling in the left lane in fairly light traffic I was forced to slam on my brakes when the car in front of me did the same. Why? Because the driver of a Jeep, CT plate 484 XGM, felt the need to slow down to a crawl so he could ILLEGALLY merge left into the car pool lane. Who does he think he is? Geno Auriemma? (In case you don't get that reference the UCONN women's basketball coach was pulled over a few years ago for pulling the exact same stunt...His excuse? He was in a hurry to get where he was going. Brilliant!) I refused to let this mental giant's ineptitude behind the wheel ruin my day, but he needs to have it pointed out to him that what he did was both illegal and dangerous. If you know him, let him know!

Commuter's Hell

Yesterday was one of those days that just provided me with so much raw material, it's hard to know where to begin. I had to chuck all my well-ordered plans in order to drive one of my charges to the hospital in New Britain. Annoyance number one: People who don't know how to park. The lines are there for a reason. You are supposed to park BETWEEN the lines, not ON them, a fact that the driver of the Nissan Rogue, CT plate 802 WSL, failed to realize. Not only did she park on the line on the driver's side, she managed to park across the line dividing the front and back parking space. A double whammy!

After work, I had to drive to Greenwich, another double whammy, traveling on I-91 and I-95 during rush hour. A word to the wise: If everyone around you has their head lights on, the street lights are on and it's almost 6:30 PM, you need to put your lights on. That's meant for you, NY plate FAV 2517.

Merging from I-91 onto I-95 is not fun on a good day, but when someone driving a BMW with CT plate 606 XUP decides to ride the "Exit Only" lane all the way to the merge and then tries to force her way into the line of traffic, it's more than a little annoying. She finally caught up to me at the Woodmont Road exit in Milford where she felt the need to brake in a line of fast moving traffic at 11 second, 9 second, 6 second and finally 2 second intervals. Do you think maybe she was a) tailgating and/or b) driving too fast?

There were a series of accidents on the NB side of I-95 and you would think that would give people pause, but it didn't, especially the driver of the Audi with NY plate AXG 4918 who zigged and zagged in and out of traffic at a high rate of speed in the area of the Westport exits.

Coming home was a lot less hair-raising. After all I'm here to post another day, and I'll be watching!

And so it goes...

I have only been writing this blog for a few days and it appears that I don't have to worry about ever running out of material.

The intersection of Main and Washington Streets in Middletown has the dubious distinction of being the first location cited twice for stupid moves by drivers. Last week it was the guy who couldn't figure out how to make a left turn without holding up an entire lane of traffic. Yesterday it was the UPS driver (K-64889) who made a left hand turn from Washington onto Main from the RIGHT lane....and yes, there were cars in the right lane.

This morning at 7:00 AM on Main Street in Portland as I sat waiting for a school bus with flashing red lights to load its passengers at the foot of Fairview Street, I watched in astonishment (but really, why was I astonished?) as a car with NY plate BXJ 957Z (I might have missed the last digit in the blur, rain and semi-darkness, but you know who you are) flew by the bus and all the other stopped cars. What part didn't you see? The big yellow bus? The line of stopped cars? The flashing red lights? Moron.

Hey, it's only 7:56 AM and I am driving to Massachusetts for a meeting today. That should provide me with plenty more pavement tales to share. Have a wonderful day....and drive carefully. Oh, yeah, and when the wipers go on, the head lights are supposed to go on. Try it.

Warning: Vanity Plates are Much Easier to Remember

My, my, the last two days have been fairly uneventful in spite of my trip to Massachusetts in the pouring rain and a trip to Manchester, CT at rush hour. And yet....Let me just single out two of my fellow travelers. A VW bearing CT plate TIN CAN cut me off on the Mass Pike Sturbridge exit ramp last evening. I'm not sure if that vanity plate refers to the driver's job in packaging or if it refers to how they feel about their car, but if they cut off the wrong person, their celestial vanity plate may well read PINE BOX.

And to the driver of CT plate 634 FLB who was ahead of me on the Glastonbury Turnpike this evening about 7:20, you have no tail lights. On second thought perhaps I have that plate wrong. It was dark AND YOU HAVE NO TAIL LIGHTS!

Big Sour Apple

You know when I hit the road for the Big Apple this afternoon I was feeling pretty good about life. Good enough that I was going to let a couple of minor irritations en route go by without comment.

Sorry, guys. At 5:23 PM my beloved RAV 4 came to a complete stop at 12th Avenue and 54th Street in Manhattan. Nothing worked. No emergency flashers, no windows, no radio, NOTHING. I had this problem once before about 14 months ago at the VA hospital in West Haven (another horror story). Anyway, I got out of my car which was in the center lane and put up the hood to alert cars that I was in distress. While there I took a look at the battery and found that the problem was the same one I had at the VA last summer. One of the battery cables had just disintegrated so I was getting no juice from the battery. I called AAA and explained to them that I knew exactly what the problem was (I believe it was a $12 repair last time) so they would be sure to bring a cable with them and then I could be on my merry way.

So I sat and waited about 22 minutes for a tow truck which quite literally came from about 300 yards away (It wasn't called 54th St. Auto for nothing). Before I recount the tale of my service from the tow truck, let me tell you what it's like to sit on the Henry Hudson Parkway with a disabled vehicle and no emergency flashers.

It's not fun.

Cars would pull up behind me, so close to my rear bumper that when they finally noticed the raised hood and the fact that I wasn't moving when the light changed, they hadn't left themselves enough room to maneuver around me. Somehow that was my fault. And their courteous reactions made that clear. Thank you, NY plate FDV 2906 for giving me the finger. Very ladylike of you. Thank you for all the horn honking, NY plate 9085, MA plate 8TT 130 and NJ plate 252 ALB.

Equally disturbing (and I hate to disclose the sex of the offenders, but the facts are the facts), 3 women sat behind me for multiple light cycles because they were so busy texting behind the wheel that they didn't notice all the cars whizzing by them on either side while my car never moved. And a special shout out to the one who finally came to and then beeped at me because she'd missed yet another green light. Oh and let's not forget the cab driver who pulled alongside of me to chastise me for not having my flashers on. At least I think that's what he was babbling about...I couldn't open the power windows to hear his helpful advice.

So the tow truck finally rolls down 54th Street and the driver tells me he can't fix the cable. He has to tow me. I deduced rather quickly from the way his eyes lit up when I told him it would be a 100 mile ride that tow truck drivers get paid extra for long hauls. We finally hit the road after he picked up his buddy, dropped his buddy off, doubled back so he could drop his keys off with someone and then took a leisurely tour of the Bronx. He wanted my opinion on everything from gay marriage to legalized prostitution to the wildlife of rural Connecticut. Actually I don't think he gave a crap about my opinion. He just wanted me to keep him awake after his late night partying in Staten Island the previous night.

We finally got to Portland, dropped the car at the repair shop and then he wanted to take me home. Luckily I had made a phone call for MY buddy to pick me up at the garage. The tow truck driver insisted on cash payment for the extra mileage although I pointed out to him that there probably wouldn't have been any extra mileage but for all his personal errands en route. When I asked for a receipt after paying him the extra money, he acted like that was a fairly ridiculous request. Luckily my friend arrived and being a much less trusting soul than I, she put her trusty cell phone camera to work. I'm not sure how I am supposed to use those photos going forward, but I guess it's good to know I have them.

So I'm home, my car is at the repair shop waiting for the guys to come in Monday morning and replace the damn cable, I didn't get to see FOLLIES and now the creepy tow truck driver knows where I live. So, because I ended up having a crappy night, it is time to call out the moron in the blue BMW, CT plate 894 YHN who was driving down I-95 in the Norwalk area like a bat out of hell, weaving in and out of traffic and tailgating. A trifecta. I hope the rest of your evening was as disappointing as mine. More importantly, I hope the need to prove your masculine prowess didn't cost anyone else their life.

Which Comes First?

It's the old chicken and egg dilemma. What comes first: the aggressive selfish driver or the flashy car?

The Portland Senior Center is located on Waverly Avenue. Waverly Avenue is a dead end street that is approximately 300 yards long....maybe a little more. If you don't happen to see the big blue sign out front that identifies the building, the proliferation of champagne colored Buick LeSabres and the like would be a dead giveaway that there were a lot of seniors in the area.

So why in hell was the driver of the blue Audi with CT plate 846 YCN flying by here at 50 miles an hour only to slam on his brakes at the intersection with Main Street? If you were looking to impress me, you succeeded--you impressed me as being a jackass.

Drinking, Driving and Just Plain Stupidity

My friend Beth and I were driving on Route 151 in East Haddam on Tuesday following a blue GMC Sierra, CT plate 4CL 331. If he wasn't drunk, someone should take away his keys just on general principle. He was moseying along as one is apt to do on those back country roads when we came to a cross street, no stop sign or stop light, and he slammed on his brakes for no apparent reason. It was only as we began moving again that we figured out why. There was a state police car waiting to make a left turn which would have required him to cross our line of traffic. Apparently the mere sight of this car which had no flashing lights or sense of urgency struck fear into this guy's heart. There could only be a couple of reasons for this.

1) He had a dead body in the back of the truck.

2) He was an illegal alien or escaped felon and/or was driving an unregistered vehicle.

3) He'd had a few pops at the local bar and his reactions were more than a little off.

I vote for the latter. A piece of advice for the driver: If you've been stupid enough to get in your truck after having a few too many, don't slam on your brakes every time you see a cop car. The driver behind you might not always have the lightning fast reflexes Beth had and a fender bender is a sure way to get the cops interested in you. In fact, the dented rear bumper you were sporting tells me that perhaps this wasn't the first time you've pulled this stunt. Knock it off before you kill someone.

And once again this morning as the bus loaded its students at the intersection of Fairview and Main Street in Portland cars just continued to fly by the bus with its red lights flashing. What is wrong with you people? I guess at this point the word of warning has to go to the students and their parents because apparently the morning commuters DO NOT GIVE A DAMN about your kids. You know, it's dark at that time of morning and ironically, that makes the flashing lights that much more obvious....but not to the oblivious.

TGIF

Last night was a bit of a trial. I had to go to Bloomfield and the roads were a mess in every direction, north, south, east and west, I-84, I-91, Route 2. It was raining and eventually sleeting and snowing (in OCTOBER!!!!!!???!!!!). And yet, except for a few minor irritations (such as the store I was going to having gone out of business) it was not as annoying as this morning's commute.

To the driver of the VW with CT plate 438 XTH who was near Ace Hardware in Middletown at 7:14 this morning: Turn signals are not optional. Try using them. It's the lever to the left of your steering wheel. And to the driver of the convertible with CT plate 937 VAU who missed their turn off of High Street in Portland: Backing up to turn into the street you apparently missed when there are cars coming down the street behind you? Not such a good idea. Go around the block next time.

Heck, it's only 9:25 AM....but at least I'm headed straight home after work today. And if you're driving on Main Street in Portland between 4 and 7 this evening, please watch out. It's time for "Trick or Treat on Main Street" and there will be literally hundreds of kids out collecting candy. Don't let your carelessness ruin what has been a really great town-wide event.

No Power Doesn't Have to Mean No Manners

This freak snowstorm certainly has thrown a monkey wrench into a lot of plans and schedules. I never did lose power but I am one of the lucky few.

I was in Massachusetts on Saturday and planned my trip according to the weather forecast, planning to be home by 5:00 when the storm was supposed to start. Mother Nature had other plans and by the time I hit the road shortly after 2:00, it was sleeting and there was full blown snow by the time I got to Worcester. Needless to say the rest of the ride home was tricky, but I have to say, people were pretty conservative, driving at a reasonable rate of speed and recognizing the poor conditions for what they were. By the time I got to Glastonbury I had already witnessed two spin outs on I-84 and then came the downed wires and trees on Routes 2, 17 and 17A. I did a bit of a spin myself on Route 17 in South Glastonbury. Black ice on an incline is a bitch, but I was going slowly enough I was able to ride it out and recover with no damage to my car or psyche.

Late Sunday I ventured out to see what the situation was around town and I was out again on Monday morning to give my friend a ride to work. Honestly I was impressed with the civility at all the intersections. It seemed like everybody recognized that we are all in the same boat and courtesy ruled the day. Until yesterday.

I took the storm refugees who were bunking with me out for a hot meal and we ventured to Wallingford to find an open restaurant. On the way home we were stopped on Route 68 in Durham, waiting to make a left turn onto Route 17 toward Middletown. Apparently our very existence annoyed the passenger in a bright yellow car, CT plate 485 XLE. As the car passed in front of us, heading south on Route 17, the female in the passenger seat felt a need to turn and give me the finger. Why? All four of us in the car are still puzzling over that. So much for letting courtesy rule.

Mother Nature can be fickle, but I would suggest we don't piss her off any more than we already have or it will be a very long winter.

Driving as a Contact Sport

I went to my sister's house in Massachusetts today. After helping her with a few odd jobs, my friend and I set out to run a couple of errands. This required covering Weston, Waltham, Arlington, Somerville, Cambridge, Wayland and Natick, all suburbs of Boston.

When I tell people that I drive into New York City, they are usually amazed that I am so brave or foolhardy, but I tell them "I used to live in Boston. Driving in New York is a piece of cake."

And while driving in New York is challenging in its own way, driving in Boston is nothing short of training for the demolition derby. The most amazing thing I ever saw in my 39 years of driving actually happened in the allegedly staid and stuffy Back Bay. I was stopped at a red light at Clarendon or Exeter Street, about to cross Commonwealth Avenue. There was a cab behind me at the light and apparently when the light changed to green, I did not move quickly enough for the cabbie. He proceeded to pass me on the right by driving up on the sidewalk to get ahead of me. Only if you know the Back Bay well can you truly appreciate that. Also in the Back Bay one day as I was riding my bike to work, a Boston driver ran a red light at

Fairfield and Commonwealth when I had the right of way. I saw my relatively short life pass before my eyes and didn't ride a bike again for over twenty years.

My friend who was riding with me today has her own issues with driving after losing her brother in a car accident. She is a nervous passenger, but trusts my driving ability enough to rein in her panic at drivers doing stupid things. But today was her first time riding around in the environs of Boston and I think it set her back a bit.

I could not take the time to jot down all the license plates and details of all the bad driving we encountered this afternoon, but I'd like to give a special shout out to the two lucky winners of today's "Dented Fender Award". First of all, the young lady driving the huge boat of a car in Teele Square in Somerville who took the opportunity to force her way from a side street into the lane of traffic simply because I was not tailgating the car in front of me could have won for that selfish boneheaded move alone. But running the red light and making the right turn on red where it clearly said "No Right Turn on Red" a few minutes later earned MA plate 22S T81 the honor in spades.

And then we come to the bald, more than middle-aged driver of the blue BMW convertible (mid-life crisis/penis substitute, anyone?) with MA plate 987 WDC on Route 20 who looked me right in the eye as he pulled out in front of me without even attempting to pretend he stopped at the stop sign. Our second winner of the day.

I love Boston and but for a twist of fate or two might have ended up living there permanently, but if the drivers in the Portland area annoy me on a daily basis, I suspect that driving in Boston every day for the last 30 years might have made me homicidal by now.

By the way, I'll be driving into New York at the end of the week. Piece of cake.

This Could Go On For Years...

The Arrigoni Bridge across the Connecticut River between Portland and Middletown is beautiful and a sight for sore eyes when heading home. Too small for the commuter traffic it now has to bear seventy-three years after it was built? Probably, but it's the only bridge we've got and I love it.

It is currently undergoing a massive update to make it safer for years to come and so traffic has been reduced to two lanes for the foreseeable future. When this project was announced you could hear the wailing and gnashing of teeth all up and down the Connecticut River Valley. I was not one of the wailers for two reasons: 1) The repairs need to be done and a little inconvenience is worth not being at the wheel of the car that could have fallen through the deck to the river below and 2) I assumed that the forced reduced speed on the bridge would lead to fewer accidents on the bridge which hold up traffic for hours on end.

I travel the bridge every morning at approximately 7:00am and since this project began several months ago I have not encountered anything but minimal delays. I know there have been one or two fender benders, at least one of which was caused by someone following too closely, but all in all things have been running smoothly. As Main Street in Portland narrows from two lanes to one at the entrance to the bridge traffic merges fairly seamlessly. Everyone knows the deal and acts accordingly. Most of the time.

This morning as we headed to the bridge, alternating cars moved into the single lane until it came to me. The woman in the Chevy with CT plate 189 WMG apparently felt there was some major advantage to be gained by cutting me off when it was clearly my turn to enter the single lane. Despite the nose of my car being ahead of hers, I backed off and let her cut me off. Obviously where she had to be was MUCH more important than where I had to be. As I crossed the bridge directly behind her I had time to ponder just what she had to gain by her action. Turns out it was easy to figure it out. She turned off the bridge onto Spring Street in Middletown exactly TWO SECONDS ahead on me. I hope she uses those two seconds wisely.

It is also worth noting that she had two stickers on the back of her car which indicated she has school age kids in sports programs. I hope she doesn't take it upon herself to teach them to drive... or anything else for that matter. Rudeness is not a family value.

If You Want To Sit In My Back Seat, Just Ask?

I've not been here for a bit, mostly because I seem to have been in a mellow mood and things on the road haven't been bugging me as much as they sometimes do. Until today.

I had to run home from work this morning to pick something up. It's about a four minute drive. As I approached the stop sign at the entrance to the high school I stopped and had to wait for someone who was exiting the school driveway. She got there first. She had the right of way. Simple, right?

Well, not so simple for the driver of the Jeep with CT plate 469 YET. As I waited at the stop sign for the woman coming out of the high school to make her left turn in front of me, I watched the Jeep in my rear view mirror and braced for impact. I know things in your mirror are closer than they appear, but I swear if this one was any closer, the driver would have been a passenger in my back seat.

Distracted Driver Alert

I need to get back to NOT watching the super bowl, but want to give a shout out to the drivers of CT 915 YWL and NY SZS 757. I know you both think you are perfectly capable of driving and talking on your cell phone, but you're not.

Nirvana

Interstate 95 northbound in Fairfield County. 1.5 miles in 22 minutes. Enough said.

When They Said Speed, He Was Listening...

Did you hear about the guy in Oregon who got stopped for speeding three times in an hour, once at 105 mph, once at 98mph and finally at 92mph? He's facing over $2000 in fines, but my favorite part of the story is his reason for driving so fast. He was on his way to a court date to face methamphetamine charges.

Sending Mixed Signals

Another fun day driving in the Boston area. Just one quick note to the driver of the Honda Pilot on Route 30 in Weston with MA plate 69M J55: If you are stopped at a light and have your left turn signal on you score one point. If you then decide not to turn, but to proceed straight ahead, look before cutting off the right lane traffic or you lose 3 points…and possibly your rear fender.

Texting, Driving and Teenage Girls

I took an hour ride across I-84 on a bus Tuesday. I'm not often a passenger in any vehicle and the elevated seat on the bus offered a different perspective on the road. I decided as the bus merged onto I-84 to observe how many people were talking on cell phones or texting while driving a minimum of 65 mph. It didn't take but a second to catch the first texter and then they passed the bus with stunning regularity. What was interesting about this little experiment was that not one of these texters or talkers was female. Every single one that I observed from Meriden to Ridgefield was male. Several of them were driving business vehicles so I would assume they were conducting business as they drove. I will admit that I have been known to occasionally take a quick call while driving, although rarely, and I have NEVER texted while driving. What amazes me about the people I observe is the brazen manner in which they break the law.

I also took a 1,000 mile road trip last week covering six states in the process. I expected to have a lot of fodder for this blog when I got home. Fortunately (or not, depending on your point of view) I didn't. The drive south was a breeze and the ride home was not bad until I reached the George Washington Bridge and miles of overnight construction in Connecticut. The start of the trip however almost set me on a rampage as I was trying to leave town and had to do the alternate merge to get on the good old (almost completed) Arrigoni Bridge.

A Toyota Tacoma truck felt the need to cut me off so he could get one vehicle length ahead of me. I find that infuriating, but was able to let it go when we got over the bridge and he had to stop at the stoplight for those heading down to Route 9 and I sailed right by to go down Main Street. "So long, sucker!"

JONAH MATRANGA

Lucky You

6 Jan 2015, 17:22, SFO, waiting to board a flight to London

Right now I'm facing an off-white wall, my feet are crossed uncomfortably, my back is pretty straight (if stiff), my vision hasn't raised in an hour or so. I've been staring at the screen of my laptop, with occasional glances at my phone, interacting with a recording of a dear friend speaking at his mom's memorial while checking Facebook so compulsively it's almost invisible and instinctive (the similarities between those words is so interesting), in between crafting an email to a booking agent I've never met in Europe somewhere, asking me if I'd like to do a month-long tour in September with two or three other oddball troubadours.

I'm wearing a Grateful Dead t-shirt I found on the street the morning after a rainstorm. It was soaked but not smelly, so I took it home and gave it a wash. Turns out it's a really soft, well-fitting shirt. There's also something very funny and satisfying to me about having found a Grateful Dead shirt in San Francisco; a city as linked with that band as tightly any band ever has been to one; a band that I have deep respect and affection for, but don't think I have bought or would buy a shirt of theirs.

I'm wearing jeans given to me a few years ago by my last serious girlfriend. They're Lucky Jeans, and for anyone that doesn't know, Lucky prints 'Lucky Me' on one side of the zipper and 'Lucky You' on the other. I can't remember which faces which way. I'm going to check. I'm self-conscious. I'm in the United Club airport lounge. I get to crash the place when I'm flying internationally cos I've flown many, many miles with them over the last 20 years. My headphones

79

are in, with no music or anything, so it just muffles the sound, but I can still tell that people are around. I usually don't like facing the wall, I like being able to survey the room. I tried it this way for fun. So unbuttoning the jeans in the fancy-ish lounge, this is one of those choices that I don't think a lot of people would make. I have equal parts pride, shame and curiosity (maybe the thing in the middle of those two things) about many choices I make, especially around social etiquette. Yea, so the inside says 'Lucky Me' and the outside says 'Lucky You'.

I got the boxer briefs underneath a while back, at this Ross Dress-For-Less on Geary between 16th and 17th, on a laundry day. I take good care of them, they're not all ratty. My socks and shoes are off. I love being barefoot as much as possible these days. Another choice I don't see a lot of people making, for better or worse.

***

6 Jan 2015, 19:11:31, waiting to take off, and the flight

I set the clock on my computer to seconds a little while ago. I imagined it might help me pay attention to moments more. When I'm at a stop light and feeling impatient, I'll count in my head to relax, remember that it's really not much time. The automobile was probably our first clue as to why we're so awful to each other on the internet. Solitary, protected, forced together onto roads but remaining stubbornly solitary. Just how we are with freeway lanes tells us so much about America.

Trading Places is on. It's astonishing how different it feels to see it now.

Doors closed, puttin this away. Stay. The needless sidewalk arrest scene. Movie's gettin real real quick. Even (and perhaps especially), when something's already made, it changes with us.

In the air. Beverage cart. Tomato juice and chamomile when I heard her offer it as an option to the guy next to me. He was so slow putting his bags up, and one fell out almost right on my head. Watching Nightcrawler on my phone. Torrented; from some film festival, apparently. My thoughts around piracy are hilariously haphazard. I like alliteration way too much. I ate a dinner's worth of snacks; 2 apples, a banana, some single-serving wrapped Monterey

Jack on single-serving wrapped crackers. Those reminded me enough of Pepperidge Farm branding that I'm pretty sure they were. One fun thing about writing all those songs last year is that it's turned my thinking, speaking and writing — and maybe especially writing — into a sort of perpetual lyric-foraging experiment. Try to catch it at thought level, before it gets hemmed in. Fenced in? Anyway, 'I'm pretty sure they were' has a nice rhythm, could make for a good hook. As could that. It was strange thinking I was done with the songs and then remembering I'd missed some early last year when I was getting my shit together, so I saved them for January 2015. 3rd, 5th, what else? Checking. 8th, 11th, British style 12, 12. Mostly birthdays, don't remember anyone talking about anniversaries or anything.

> While my friends are having anniversaries
> I'm hangin round the internets
> Wishing for weirdos like me
>
> Why aren't we dancing all the time
> Holding hands and giggling
> When did we decide that being safe and sane
> Had to look like suffering
>
> Every time I go out to a party
> I end up in the corner with a magazine
> Everybody talkin about nothin
> Like it's everything
>
> And I'm wishing for weirdos like me

That arrived a couple weeks back. I think I got sad when I stopped making them every day. Felt good to feel it, not try to fix it. Also fun to realize there were more to do. I loved how easily one arrived today. It's to Ruth, always neat to make them for people I know. I missed her birthday (said hi on Facebook and that I'd see her soon).

Oof, this is tiring. Gonna try watching while I write. Remember to sleep when it's time.

Oh yea, I turned off Trading Places. Couldn't take a flick with voices that good getting censored, and in the process overdubbed terribly. It's just about impossible to replace the poetry of well-executed curse words.

This is something I can learn from. It'd be fun to time the scenes without words, how they tell the story that way. I want this movie to be beautiful. I want to give someone else room to roam that way, but I want to be let in to that part, too, so I can learn.

Wait, what just happened? What crime scene are they at? Might not be able to write well while watching. Fun to stumble into four double yous.

It's neat they're using the video camera so much, too. I know I want that to be a character.

My phone is being propped up to a decent viewing angle by a banana on some magazines. I had to put the one with the more matte texture on top to grip the side of the phone.

Rewinding.

I remember telling Hannah to wait for the movie to unfold, that there would be an answer, a resolution, if she was patient and watched closely. Everything I've — so much that I've said to her has ended up being what I believe. The process of trying to pass that to her, to give her reasonable answers and critical thinking tools, has helped me articulate my take on so much. And sometimes the way she's said it has become the way I see it. What'd she say today when we were having that great talk? Oh yea, that she just likes people, that she sees them as little kids. She's more kind and understanding than I am. Makes sense, her world wasn't as scary and chaotic growing up.

I didn't miss any big — oh wait, he's filming a crib. They didn't show inside. Interesting. He's chasing even creepier shit and taking his time, all alone. More brazen and creative. Leaving as the cops arrive. His matter-of-fact blunt schtick works well. The co-lead is fantastic. It's fun seeing a new face.

Do I want to star in this thing? Maybe I have to, but the idea of writing the songs for someone else to sing and building a character I don't need to play is pretty exciting, too. Like songwriting. And what about my nagging lack of interest in the idea of aspiring? Ah, when the question marks start appearing is where it starts getting boring for me.

This car chase is riveting and this movie's meta is really clever. I'm not sure the cops would have been that far behind given all this. This death scene is a little much, drifting over the drama edge. High standards set.

The control dynamic is gonna be so important to do right.

The tone has gone a bit screwy. Reel it in. Tough to get back from being lost.

I think the movie could be structured by songs. I'm so scared of the script. Mostly the talking.

Ah, the movie's ending. Didn't quite pay off. Ironic. Also, I thought he was gonna stage a murder or something, as in perpetrate it or facilitate it somehow. Would that have been too much? I think it's time to sleep. This is a strange chronicling. Is that a word?

Damn, this ice cream sandwich is too frozen. The meal was good. I think I'm off the vegan meals. The desserts always suck.

This is a ten hour flight.

22:22:08 PST

Eyes closing. I'll have to pee sometime. Or the guy next to me. Lights just went out in the plane. Watching through lowered lids. These protagonists are my age. So is the soundtrack. Clash. Pixies. Stomach. Excess. I was gonna go with Farrah, they went with Tiegs. It's be neat if that was really how it's spelled. I want to be mumbling this. It'd be fun to mess with mumbling and dictation. Mimic that this way. Model.

05:20:25 PST

Pretty sure that means 13:20:25 in London. Only hesitation is learning recently that for some small window of time the daylight savings thing shifts it. I guess we do it on different days?

I've got one foot on top of the other; my left on top of my right. The left one is restless, the right one kind of on its side. I always have to shake out the right one, not sure why I'd do it this way. My stomach feels a bit bloated, eyes bleary, body that odd combo of dry/damp, muggy/chilly that seems to be the by-product of a long flight, maybe especially overnight. Would've been neat to measure body temperature and blahblah over all the years, see if I could see patterns. Kinda like I wish I'd taken a picture of every bed I've ever slept in, or saved all my boarding passes. The beds thing could've been really great, just for sheer volume, and I'm sure some of the shots would've been poetic. Bathrooms too, even? I guess any room or area would do, it's the repetition that matters.

Time to write a movie. Time to type that a lot and see if I actually do it.

***

Dammit, almost made it to bed without seeing another white, would-be progressive friend decrying the scary internets for being hypersensitive about race. Ah, white fragility. You're killer. Fellow white people, it's really pretty simple: If you're more concerned with being 'unfairly' called a racist than about centuries of bloody, horrific oppression (that is continuing right... now), you're doing it wrong.

G'nite.

Love,

Tired (in so many ways) me.

***

I dreamt about a woman in England
Who gave her tickets for Serena's match
To her Black maid
All the games we've played

Every time we've vanished
And every time we've stayed
All the games we've played

Starting and stopping
Rising and dropping
Robbering and copping

***

Pretty gross how they're trotting him (megastar-of-the-moment Chris Pratt) out as their show pony. Idolatrous and blasphemous, even.

As for 'liberal Christians', serious question: what does that mean to the people here? Here's what I mean: I sing at a place called Glide. The pastoral team is serious about their scripture and they consistently deconstruct it in really interesting, challenging ways. No one seems too caught up in evolution, dinosaurs, virgin births, resurrections, taking scripture that simply and literally etc. We have a choir filled with transgender people, gay people, all colors, all shapes & sizes. The church is in the heart of one of the most underserved, impoverished neighborhoods in the city. The focus is on serving the poor, combating racism, and overall social justice. I myself am a Jewish, Buddhist-ish, atheist-ish weirdo, and everyone seems to sincerely love me and appreciate me, with no closet proselytizing. Is that what you mean? Cos I'll admit it, I'm kinda tired of 'liberal' Christians that have nice-sounding rhetoric, but then have the same ugly, ignorant white/straight biases that give the religion the horrible rep it sometimes deserves.

So, yr (honest) thoughts?

(Never sent)

Hi. Another coupla weeks gone by. 2 months since the fateful, fucked up eve. I'm through the exhausted and heartbroken part, and just kinda empty/numb (which feels horrible, but more peaceful than waiting). Like I wrote about before, if there can't be easier forgiveness/reconciliation about such things (that will happen in any friendship/life) and some sense of shared accountability/reflection, I just can't imagine feeling safe (ah the irony) in our friendship, since I'm sure I'll screw up again in one way or another, as we all do, and I don't enjoy walking on eggshells and/or being held at a distance. At this point, I pretty much think you owe me an apology, but I'm not holdin my breath. I still love you somethin fierce, probably always will, forever grateful for so much... but this just isn't working for me.

***

I'm worried that someone has stolen my daughter's phone and is writing to me from it as if it were her. In a related matter, what do I want to do today? I want to write an email telling people to buy my things and come to see me saying that I'm grateful that they do. Why do I keep not doing this? So many years later, and I'm still writing the journal entry, and I'm still aware the questions are themselves clues, and even if I figured it out countless times, it still remains a mystery.

I'm having trouble figuring out any good reason to do anything, as long as I somehow keep enough money trickling in to keep myself and my daughter safe and comfortable in some modest way.

ROOSEVELT CHAMPION III

We're messy as a riot
Kinda less worthwhile
Everybody quiet
Walk in single file

Bitterness as bravery
Saccharine and slavery
Why are we surprised
Every time we figure out we're not free

Roosevelt Champion
What happened to you?
Tell me everything
I wanna hear you

Single pour and nails
Riding off the rails
10, 9, 8, Red Sails
Short memory, short memory
We made a big machine, and this is the exhaust
I'm trying really hard and feeling really lost
Tell me what you need tell me what you felt
I really wanna know, Roosevelt Champion

***

I'm still sad sometimes
That I'm not in Rolling Stone
I still have this nagging fear
That I'm gonna die alone

These aren't things that I want to say too loud
But I want to say them to you
I want to have you near me
Watching me go through

***

SERIOUS QUESTION(S):

I like true stories the best. This is not about me judging Chris Kyle, nor anyone here. It's about me being heartbroken that we created this horrifying, violent mess where people aren't thought of as people, and where gazillions are spent glorifying and obfuscating the ugly realities of ourselves and our nuts human culture, rather than being real with each other and seeing where that gets us. All too often in the name of God™ and/or Freedom™, as if it could get any more tragically ironic. Serious question: why do we worship violence?

***

I'm Jewish. In 1938 in Poland, it might be the time to say #JewishLivesMatter, because according to that culture's laws and everyday life realities, they didn't matter as much. Now, at least in the US (and in the UK as well, as far as I can tell), that's just not the case. In the current cultural climate, Jewish or not, I'm white, and I receive many cultural benefits for that. I can still speak up about the complexities of being Jewish (or anything else) in any number of ways while still acknowledging that my life matters more in the eyes of our culture than many people with darker skin than me.

***

It's perfect but I'm speaking this into my phone as I walk down the street. I will leave all the strange typos from where my phone doesn't understand me. I just saw the movie *Her.* It is the most emotionally evocative thing I've experienced in a while, I think. Intellectually, as well. Aside from all of the logistical things we've got going on, like I dwindling resources and I dwindling oxygen and the way that we're living unsustainably, this game of intellect that we've created this game of words and all that, we're going to lose. Of course we are. And trying to turn nature into sequences and patterns and codes and languages, we make ourselves irrelevant, and we don't seem to be aware of that. Our bodies, which is all we really are, of course, are really good at being a part of all this. Our brains, even our whole skill of time, just can't keep up with this new system we're trying to make. I'm sure that at some point it seems like a really good idea to lift ourselves above the animal kingdom with their words and their weapons, but it's not going to work out very well for us in the end. And that's okay, because we'll go on as we always have. Matter will still matter, so to speak. All this said, the moves the movie please be feeling a little more free to leave all of this behind I love these words that I'm reaching for to try to talk about this. I think my sentences are starting to make less and less cents, because I'm forgetting to say the punctuation marks. And of course, since sounds like cents sounds like science. I'm so sensitive, ha ha. I'll bet there's some great equation to be drawn up about how my phone's hearing, how well it can understand me, is increasing just as fast as my own hearing is decaying. Faster. Faster. Faster. This is creepy and meta- and fun. I think I'll write more this way in the future. Thanks for listening. I was talking to the phone, not you. But I'm happy you're here too, ha ha.

***

Tour definitions aside, if you're not spending most of your waking hours writing, recording, playing shows, keeping in touch with people about those things, and all the other stuff that goes with all that... then you're not a 'musician'. You're someone doing something else and playing music once in a while. And there's nothing wrong with that, of course; playing music is great fun no matter what... just keepin it real. Hi from the 500 mile drive between Salt Lake City and Denver. 3000-ish shows, 20-ish albums, 20-ish years. Yup. 'Sup.

***

I want to celebrate your independence, I just have a hard time witnessing it. I don't want to see the food in the room, and the mess, and the hours spent lying in bed. You know I have trouble with that stuff. I want you to have those moments, I really do. I'm just terrified that you're going to follow down the stairs everyone else I love is gone there. I love you so much and I'm so scared that you're going to turn out like everyone else left so much. I have secretly wished to never stop being the father that goes to the track meet with the video camera, and I've secretly wished to be done, to know that I did it right, to know that you made it out okay. So now, when you're coming back home clearly looking for guidance and support, I just don't know what to do. I just don't know what the right move is.

***

I just want to be at the ocean
I'm tired of all of our words
Air and our bodies happened
Every time you heard what you heard

***

There is so much freedom in the realization that no one cares or listens, really. Then I can just get on with making stuff. Also, keeping that truth in mind is the thing most likely to facilitate the creation of anything worth listening to or caring about.

***

Here's a watercolor that I made with Eric that day we took the walk. He had brought the kit. He said he liked painting at different moments he wanted to remember. At first I was just gonna sit and wait while he did his, then I figured I'd give it a try. It was really relaxing and sweet to do something I've hardly done before, trying to get the essence of the moment down on paper. It's me & him (the two little dots on the dark line, which was the plank of wood we were sitting on) at Baker beach, looking out at the ocean and the hills, sun setting. Two people in the world. I think of me & you, I think of you & yr boyfriend, all of us different duos making it through, tiny dots on the big beach of the world, this life. I told Eric the story of you & me making the chalk lines on the sidewalk to show yr boyfriend the way to find you. I told him of my silly surprise when you & I reached the entrance to Baker and I realized it was time for me to go. I had gotten so wrapped up in the activity that I'd forgotten about that part. Then, walking back, I saw him, he saw me, across the street. At first, we just exchanged glances and waves. Then, as he was heading down the street, I turned, asked him to take good care of you. He said he would. I really hope he has and does. No matter what happens, I also remember you talking to me in the car after some sort of breakup thing. You were talking about the memories of sitting in the backseat of our car, with whomever you were talking about, as I drove you both somewhere. I offered the idea that your memories are yours to keep forever, whether you keep knowing the person you made them with or not. That offer stands.

***

And so I was sitting there watching Baby Mama, at the melancholy part when everything's gone wrong and you're just not sure how it will all get right, and I was imagining a song of mine in there. I was thinking about not being successful enough, about not having my music in movies, about failing at music. (I hadn't thought about it like that). And then it washed over me, as it has lately, just yesterday even as I was headed to David's wondering how the album would turn out. Both times, I realized laughing, smiling, in tears, that music is fun. I just love to make it. It's just fun. For someone that loves words so much, I have trouble writing it out. But there it is. Just try to -- no, don't try to hold on to the moment -- just breathe into it. Again and again. As long as it takes. Feel the fun.

***

You are no different than me. At the same time, you are something that simply doesn't exist yet. I am dying and being born at every moment, just like you. Do you look back upon right now as a sad time? Do you remember waking up slow and cloudy? Do you

90

remember the lifting of the veil when the ocean hit your skin? Are you still writing to your future self? Wait, I know all these things. I know you. My work is beyond books and mantras. It's about simple awareness, acceptance and action. So is yours.

Keep going. Just keep going. I will too.

JIM BREGA

The Wright Stuff
Encounters with Frank Lloyd Wright and Others on a Trip Across America

9/21/2008

Dodging panhandlers and navigating closed streets, finally found our downtown Cleveland hotel. It appears to be in the most deserted section of Cleveland: streets lined with empty storefronts and office towers, early skyscraper period, 100% of which are being reconstructed but with preservationist's approach. Beautiful architectural details abound. Every office building has a group of four or five smokers standing in front of it taking their cigarette break; they manage somehow to give the impression that they're the only inhabitants of the buildings, of the city. No one else comes in or goes out while we watch. Overall effect is that Armageddon happened and smokers were the only ones spared.

Main event today was a visit to the Rock and Roll Hall of Fame, building designed by I.M. Pei. Another pyramid (like his 1984 addition to the Louvre in Paris), most spacious below ground level. Upper floors cramped and almost unusable.

Museum has an interesting collection of costumes displayed on mannequins; their scale suggests that almost every famous Rock performer is four and a half feet tall.

The level of detail on the costumes for bands that routinely play in stadium shows is surprising. Particularly impressive are the hand-camouflaged silver/brown shoes for Aerosmith. Nice stuff for Madonna by Jean-Paul Gaultier. Surprisingly feminine outfits for

Jimmy Hendricks: bias ruffles down front, sheer "jacket" over printed shirt, velvet pants. It becomes apparent that a lot of what appears to be "thrown together" onstage is professionally designed and carefully constructed by costume houses.

Overall impression of the R&RHOF is of chaos—not in a creative way—and cold. Had to wear fleece pullover even though it was 70 degrees outside. Main themes seemed to be:

• R&R grew out of an appropriation of black, country, and western roots by the white market.

• R&R is a product of youthful rebellion that became an iconoclastic art form that flies in the face of conventional society and revels in insult and outrage. Yay!

Good Mexican food for dinner at nearly deserted sports bar near hotel.

9/23/2008

Leaving the unimpressive Cleveland Botanical Garden, stumbled across the Frank Gehry-designed Peter B. Lewis Building which houses the Weatherhead School of Management at Case Western Reserve University. Stainless steel roofline suggests a Brobdingnagian-scaled pile of used giftwrap. Tilted brick façade fails to integrate Gehry's building with those adjoining. Security graciously allowed us to step into the lobby; that was enough to make us feel claustrophobic in spite of what the building's description calls "a soaring space." In my opinion, it does not soar. The design is all about the drama of the exterior.

9/24/2008

Left South Bend headed toward Chicago. Initial impression as we approached: smog, congestion, poverty—typical large American city I guess.

Found our way to Oak Park to visit Frank Lloyd Wright home and studio. Wait time: 2 hours, so took the self-guided audio walking tour of the area surrounding the home he lived in from 1889 to 1913 and where he executed 24 commissions. Lots of variety documenting the development of more and more modern ideas. Many stunning examples of design. Especially liked the exterior of the Unity Temple—a Unitarian Universalist church included on the tour. Lots of echoes of Hollyhock House/Olive Hill in LA.

FLW's home and studio were as usual with his interiors: impressive attention to detail in what ends up feeling like a doll house as a result of cramped spaces and low ceilings. (FLW designed spaces to suit himself, even in clients' homes. He was 5'8½" tall.) The children's playroom on the second floor was the only one with a reasonable sense of space, and even that room with its barrel ceiling and elaborate sconces (it doubled as a private theatre) had to be adapted to accommodate his grand piano: the sounding board protrudes through the wall into an adjacent stairwell.

Decorations (capitals, friezes, figural statues) all interesting and emphasizing aspects of truth, knowledge, strength, etc. The octagonal library's exterior decoration is bands of repeated small octagons, each one rotated x degrees so that the angle of one bisects the straight edge of the next. Ingenious! The floral light screens over the dining room table and in the playroom still anchor the design style firmly in the Victorian period.

Would be remiss if I did not mention that the married Wright had to leave Oak Park because he entered into an affair with the wife of one of his clients.

9/25/2008

Today given over to exploring Chicago on foot, which began in Millennium Park with Frank Gehry's "serpentine bridge" leading to an outdoor pavilion. A web of metal struts form a roof suspended above the lawn, the seating area for informal performances. Nearby a fountain consisting of two vertical slabs on which faces are projected. Each image eventually spits real water into the fountain.

One fascinating object in the park is Anish Kapoor's sculpture "Cloud Gate," which the public has renamed "the bean." Meticulously constructed, there are no seams, rivets, or other construction clues in its perfect, mirrored stainless steel form.

Enjoyed encountering Picasso and Calder sculptures on public plazas mixed in with the modern office towers; large open spaces planted with lawn, trees, and flowers with Adirondack chairs scattered about—lovely, and everything Cleveland would like to be. Left the city by a much nicer route than that by which we'd arrived.

9/26/2008

Got on the 11am tour of Johnson Wax headquarters in Racine,

Wisconsin. Tours of the Wright-designed administration building, still in daily use as Johnson's world headquarters, and parking garage very tightly regulated, so it's difficult to roam or examine things too closely... Which didn't keep a group of 3 French tourists from blithely ignoring the guide's instructions to stop taking pictures and stop wandering off—a safety issue as a number of the buildings on site are still used by JW for research and light manufacturing. After the tour, the male in the group had to be removed from the industrial area by security guards. He was carrying a small drawing tablet on which I was able to glimpse some nice charcoal sketches before he was hauled away.

The Johnson Wax administration building interior: Smaller than expected, but still impressive. Famed "lily pads" enchant in person as they do in photos. Impact lessened by major repair being carried out everywhere, especially in lobby/reception. No access to the research tower; closed for retro-fitting to meet modern fire regulations. In general, Wright's structures still look startlingly modern but somehow lost or out-of-place in juxtaposition with the adjacent manufacturing complex.

One interesting detail: FLW died in 1958, but his firm,Taliesin Associated Architects, was hired to create a structure on the JW grounds to house a small museum and a theatre in which to show the short film "To Be Alive." Both had originally been created for the Johnson Wax pavilion at the 1964 World's Fair, and I remember seeing it there when my family drove cross-country to attend. Hard to believe that was almost 45 years ago!

Unfortunately, the building created in Racine by Taliesin Associates was uninteresting: a box with the original saucer of the theatre plopped on top of it.

On to Taliesin!

9/27/2008

There's a category of restaurant that Wisconsonites refer to as a "supper club;" this revealed to us by the desk clerk at the Motel 8 in Kenosha, near Racine, in answer to the question, "Where's a good place to eat around here?" After declining her first two suggestions—Pizza Hut, McDonalds—we were offered the elegant-sounding third alternative. It conjured memories of Astaire/Rogers movies, or one of the episodes of "I Love Lucy" in which she manages to talk herself into the show at Ricky's club. Was it possible that some version of club culture, circa 1930, survived among the Wisconsin dairy farms? We had to go.

It turns out that a supper club, Wisconsin-style, is a restaurant that serves steaks and fish and has a bar. And, if you ignore the brown lettuce in the salad, the brown skin on the lime in the watered-down gin and tonics, the saltine cracker appetizers served with "spread" (cream cheese mixed with chives), and the cigarette-smoke-saturated interior still sporting last year's Christmas decorations, it is pretty elegant despite lacking a floor show. We had some language problems negotiating our order. Me to waitress: "How is the fish cooked?" Waitress to me, "I don't know." Several seconds of blank stares pass between us. Waitress: "Would you like me to find out?" The mahi-mahi, grilled, turned out to be quite good.

9/28/2008

We had a reservation for the 10:15 Taliesin tour this morning. The bus driver had to be at least 80. Our guide was Melinda, great granddaughter of the owner of the lumber mill that provided FLW with much of the materials used in building Taliesin.

Tour started at what had been a boarding school run by FLW's two aunts, now part of the still-operating school for architecture. I can't add much to the many photos and words already produced in re: these buildings, except to say that there was wood rot and deterioration everywhere.

To experience the house was thrilling, overlooking the usual discomfort of low ceilings. Rooms were more expansive than usual; the views of the Wisconsin countryside were outstanding. There's little colored glass incorporated into the leaded windows as it's not needed to enhance the experience. Overall, successfully evokes the spirit of an Italian villa, influenced by FLW's visit to Italy.

Here is one place where FLW's interest in integration with Nature is apparent. Taliesin (Welsh for "shining brow") is situated just below the top of the hill on which it's built, so that from the back garden the house is invisible. It's a wonderful effect. Also wonderful: the integration of Asian art—screens, rugs, ceramics, etc. Not so wonderful: the overly close supervision during the tour that prevented us from pausing to admire or absorb much of the exterior.

One anecdote from tour guide: FLW designed furniture for all of his interiors—including Taliesin—that was famously uncomfortable. Late in life, fed up, he reportedly complained, "I am tortured by my own furniture!" He eventually replaced the chairs in the sitting-rooms at Taliesin with over-stuffed armchairs from a Chicago department store.

Note: All of what we see today at Taliesin, with the exception of Wright's studio, is the result of a re-building following a murderous 1914 arson attack by a deranged employee. His studio, with all his letters and plans, was saved from the flames by his injured foreman. His mistress, for whom he had built the place, her two children, and a dozen employees were all brutally murdered. Wright himself was not present during the attack.

9/29/2008

Arrived in Rapid City, SD in preparation for visit to Mt. Rushmore. Stopped for lunch—enticed by highway signs seemingly every quarter mile for the last 300 miles—in Mitchell, SD, home of the Corn Palace. A real tribute to kitsch, exterior of the building completely covered in decoration made from various varieties and colors of corn. Reminds one of the style often referred to as tramp art.

Notes from the road (so far):

Best gas station name: Kum & Go

Best business sign (painted 3 ft. high): 24-hour Toe Service

We spent all of Monday at Mt. Rushmore National Park. The Black Hills scenery is spectacular, especially numerous stone fingers that stick up—not sure whether due to earthquake or volcanic activity followed by erosion. The sculpture itself is much more impressive than I thought it would be, and can be approached via a trail/boardwalk that goes to the base of the debris pile. Twists and turns provide different views of specific heads. Biggest surprise was seeing lines suggesting spectacles on TR, only because I'd never noticed them before.

In a small clearing about halfway along the trail, a Native American park service employee had a hide from a recently butchered buffalo staked out. She was explaining how every part of the animal was used by NA hunters.

• Un-tanned hide dried hard and could be used to make storage

boxes
- Un-tanned tail used as fly swatter
- Hollow horn became drinking cup, powder horn, or container to carry fire from one camp to the next
- Ligaments were dried, pulled apart into sinews, and used for laces or ties
- Hollow hooves were hung on strips outside of teepee for use as a "doorbell"
- Ribs were used as sled runners; other bones as tool handles, scrapers, etc.
- Tanned hides were used for clothing, teepee covers, rugs, etc.

9/30/2008

Here's an example of exactly what I hoped to encounter when we set off on this trip: in the middle of nowhere we saw an exit sign for Devil's Tower National Monument, and took an unplanned turn. 30 minutes later we were at the tower, which is 1250 feet in elevation and soars 820 feet above the visitor's center. According to geologists, the tower was formed by streams of molten igneous rock flowing through granite tubes and forming 5-, 6-, or 7-sided crystals. 50 million years of erosion have left the tower free of the softer surrounding layers of soil and stone.

Best advertising sign in Jackson Hole, WY: Hole Juice
Best business sign in Utah: Pop Food Worms

10/11/2008

We arrive at Taliesin West near Scottsdale, AZ in time for our noon tour. The attitude among the guides is much more relaxed than it had been at Taliesin East; we're invited to take pictures both inside and out during the tour.

The buildings were again built just below the top of a hill, with a beautiful view for many miles across the desert…interrupted by electrical towers and power lines that run across the property. These were installed during FLW's lifetime, and so frustrated him that he raised the height of the windows in the rooms facing the lines so that they aren't visible when sitting in the rooms.

FLW's concept for TW was that it is a camp. Although the buildings cover an estimated 45,000 square feet and are built of stone and concrete (it's said he wanted to use materials that wouldn't burn), many ceilings are canvas. At TW, the concrete that was one of his favored building materials is readily visible as mortar between large local boulders. FLW treated the local rocks, some with prehistoric petroglyphs, as centerpieces or totems, and placed them near the entrances to the buildings, much as he used sophisticated cast concrete planters in his commercial and residential projects.

Overall sense is of rusticity, whether by intent and developing temperament or because of lack of money for more sophisticated buildings.

While FLW was alive, he initiated the tradition of spending the spring and summer at Taliesin East and the fall and winter at Taliesin West. The entire household, including the students in the architecture school, would move as well, and would provide most of the labor that went into building Taliesin West.

10/13/2008

We had an appropriate welcome to California this morning: an earthquake. It made me think about our visit a few days ago to Chaco Canyon, an extensive prehistoric building complex in the middle of the New Mexico desert. One of the large structures we saw there had been designated as unstable by the National Park Service. They'd made the decision not to shore it up, to let nature take its course. Though today's quake was nowhere near the canyon, the NPS policy makes me wonder about how we value things. Would we let Taliesin West fall if it were threatened? The prehistoric architects of Chaco Canyon were just as skilled, in their own way, as FLW's students, yet we might value their work less because we don't know who they were or why they built. On the other hand, maybe the NPS is right: we shouldn't interfere with natural processes. Everything man creates is someday likely to fall, or be replaced.

We'd set off from Farmington, NM on 10/9, having spent the night in the Days Inn on the edge of town. Like all the motels in Farmington, its parking lot is surrounded by a 10-foot chain link fence with coiled razor wire on top. Signs warn against leaving valuables in the car, so we'd moved all the computer equipment, cameras, etc. from the back of the Escape to our room.

We easily found the obscure turn-off, soon passed on to the 13 miles of dirt road leading to Chaco Culture National Historical Park. As the driver, I struggled initially with the eroded, washboard road. I thought we might have to travel the whole way at 20mph with the car heaving violently from side to side and front to back, but after being passed by a small sedan doing about 45 and seeing his wheels bouncing like time-lapse yo-yos, we realized that the secret is to drive fast, so that the wheels don't sink into the 4-inch ruts but bounce from the top of one to the top of the next. This is a really exciting way to travel; with little tire contact with the ground, steering is nearly useless. After a few minutes my hands were cramped from gripping the steering wheel and I was sweaty all over. John and I took turns seeing who could scream the loudest as we flew around curves hoping we wouldn't meet any cars coming the other way. At least we were now travelling at about 40mph and making good time.

According to the NPS, Chaco Canyon hosts the densest and most exceptional concentration of pueblos in the southwest. Nobody knows who the builders were or why they chose to build there, though the structures' alignment with astronomical phenomena suggests, as it does at Stonehenge, that it may have some religious significance. Analysis of trash piles suggests that no one actually lived in the main complex. There are 50 or so small settlements scattered across the valley nearby—possibly caretakers. The Chetro Ketl site, combined with Pueblo Bonito next to it, formed the "downtown" section of the city. The structures were built using sandstone quarried from the top of the surrounding canyon walls, presumably because it's harder and more durable than the sandstone at lower elevations. The builders were highly sophisticated and skilled and obviously observed a rigid aesthetic, even though they had only stone tools to work with. Right-angled shapes (exterior corners, windows, doors, etc.) were extremely precise, though circles (kivas) were more approximate. Logs for roof supports (some 2 feet in diameter) were brought to the site from 20 to 60 miles away.

The complexes were built in a "D" shape, with the curved wall enclosing a plaza. There are few petroglyphs, distinguishing the culture from that of the Pueblos. The whole place seems to have been constantly expanded and remodeled. There are no explanations for why the site was abandoned in about 1250 AD; one speculation is that the highly structured society that would have been required to construct it over 300 years was torn apart by some sort of political strife. Seeing the craftsmanship, sophistication, and ingenuity of the builders, it's difficult to understand why they never felt the need to develop a written language (unlike Aztec and Inca civilizations shortly after) that could have helped us understand them. Similar "Great Houses" are scattered across an estimated 60K square miles of Arizona, New Mexico, Utah, and Colorado. My feeling is that this was a civilization that rivaled the size and power of Mexican pre-Columbian civilizations, but because of the lack of a written language we know almost nothing about it.

One example of foresight employed at Taliesin West that the Chacoans never thought of: the deep eaves and covered walkways of TW prevent the drifting sand from penetrating the interiors of the rooms. Most of what is visible at Chaco Canyon today has been reclaimed from the sand by archeologists and others, but every day the desert is doing everything in its power to cover it up again.

TOM CARTER

Peruvian Amazon

My month-long trip to the Peruvian Amazon was made possible by my travelling companion, Mike Gilmore, an ethnobotanist who has worked with the Maijuna people for a decade and a half. Our initial destination, Iquitos, is the largest city on earth that cannot be reached by road or rail, accessible only by flight or river voyage.

We arrive via overnight flight from Miami to Lima and a connection to Iquitos. Waking to the rising sun while flying over the snow-covered Andes Mountains is a wondrous experience, but our destination was even more magical.

Iquitos is very much locked in the past, it feels like a Gabriel Garcia Marquez novel. One of the few signs of the 20th Century is the internal combustion engine, but even the vehicles are quaint and antiquated. Almost all are three-wheeled motorcycles called motokaros. Most are taxis with a bench behind the driver but some are set up for cargo, with small pick-up truck-like beds. They buzz around the town in utter chaos, with little concern for lanes, pedestrians, or the omnipresent Peruvian hairless dogs, which have free range of the city. The lively music emanating from stores, restaurants, and houses manages to cut through the din of the motokaros. The tropical trees filling the city's many parks and squares counterbalance the chaotic energy of the streets to give the city a chill vibrancy. Unless they are piloting a motokaro, the people seem to be in no hurry. They are friendly and easy-going, but each block contains at least one person offering to sell something. These peddlers always cheerfully accepted my lack of interest.

Iquitos is also a city where you can find anything for sale, whether it is legal or not. I was offered drugs, women, animal skins, and many more mundane products. Some tourists come to get a taste of the jungle through shorts forays into the rainforest. Others come to experience ayahuasca, a psychotropic herbal concoction used by some tribes for healing and seeing the divine and by tourists for recreation. The road from the airport to the hotel was lively with traffic and street performers, including three guys on very high unicycles juggling machetes. Between the trio, they kept around eight machetes in the air at any given time.

***

The owner of the hotel, who was expecting Mike, greeted us and proudly showed us the pool, meeting room, and breakfast area. After a quick dip in the bug-covered pool and a shower, we set out on our many errands to prepare for the trip up the river with the students, who arrive in two days. Jake, a filmmaker documenting the Maijuna, gets here tomorrow. A day later we will be joined by a group of students from George Mason University, who will travel with us to the first of two remote Maijuna villages.

As soon as we were out in the city on foot, I get swept up by Iquitos' unique blend of ease and energy. I soon realized that the motokaros drivers and passengers are probably already half an hour late for whatever they're heading to do.

Back at the hotel we were met in the lobby by a stream of Mike's friends and associates: Victor Hugo, who runs a number of businesses and will provide the boat for our trip to Sucasari; Gerardo, who works for an NGO in Iquitos; Roosevelt (pronounced Roosbell), president of the Maijuna tribes; and Sebastian, "mayor" of Sucasari and very close friend to Mike whom everyone calls Sheba or Shebaco. Sheba and I shared a motokaro taxi down to the docks to check things out and call Sucasari on short wave radio. I tried to use my Spanish as we ran around the city planning for the first leg of our adventure.

Sheba, Geracho, Mike and I went to dinner at Kiki Riki, which serves chicken cooked on skewers, along with either fries or platanos. A massive plate of half a bird and a pile of platanos costs roughly four dollars.

After dinner Mike, Sheba and I met Mike's former student Elvis and his friends at a bar/hostel that literally floats in the part of the Rio Itaya that used to be part of the Amazon before the latter was diverted. On the other side of the city is the Rio Nanay, which is generally wider than the Itaya, except for the marshy wide section east of Iquitos that used to be the Amazon. The city sits on the V of land where the two rivers come together and flow into the Amazon. The mighty Amazon is already around two miles wide at this point, even though it's far closer to its Peruvian headwaters than to its mouth across the continent.

To reach the bar we walked to a street that ended atop the river bank. As we walked down some steep, rickety wooden stairs the sounds of the city above disappeared and were replaced by trancy Afrobeat music. The floating structures of Camiri across a wobbly floating gangplank were illuminated by a string of white lights. We sat under the stars on a docklike structure tied to the main bar structure. The music was satellite radio from a U.S. college station. The mix of third and first world perfectly captured this strange cityThe men and women who work with Elvis are also botanists and were telling me all about the jungle. One of them is working on English, and Elvis is in school in the states. But my Spanish is definitely improving already. By last night I could make out about a third of what people were saying and was able to speak some simple sentences.

***

I woke up on Tuesday morning and took a run through the city and along the river. I love watching cities wake up. The streets were already humming with the ubiquitous motokaros. They drive like madmen through the streets, which are--thankfully--all one way. But they have as many lanes as can squeeze in, and the drivers are competitive, so it is like a Formula One track.

To escape the streams of motokaros this morning, I ran down to and along the river. There are some parts of the banks overlooking the river that are parklike, and sometimes there is a road along the bank, but at some spots the perpendicular streets dead-end at the steep declivity. I ran as close to the water as I could. The Itaya is very wide and shallow near the banks, with small islands and hammocks of growth. It has a tropical delta look and was beautiful at sunrise.

I also saw lots of kids walking to school, mostly in uniform. Even the little ones as young as four tend to walk by themselves. This is a city where the kids and the dogs run free. At one point a brigade of people with buckets and primitive homemade brooms came walking towards me. On my return I saw them all lined up at a square getting scoops of detergent from a municipal worker. They would then hose off a section of the sidewalk or street and scrub it down with their soapy brooms.

The street sweepers were part of a large group of people spilling over a wall at the top of the bank. Below was an entire shanty town called Belen built of palm thatch on stilts. Iquitos just experienced a flood of 100-year levels, so all of those houses were underwater a week or so ago. The area is still filled with detritus, and the residents are busy cleaning up their huts.

On the return run I tried to find ways to stay by the water longer but came upon a dead end. I looked through a door and saw the street on the other side and a brick wall along one side. Thinking that it was a narrow alleyway I started running through only to discover that it was a corridor and that what I thought were shop entrances opposite the wall were rooms in someone's house. The occupants were as bewildered as I, and I turned and ran back out before they could figure out why a gringo was running down their hall.

We spent all day buzzing around town meeting with various people and preparing for the rest of our trip. Some of the guys went to buy all the food and supplies for the students and send those on a boat up to Sucasari, our first village. Jake arrives today and the students tomorrow, then we leave for the village on Thursday. I am really eager to get into the jungle!

Later in the morning, Mike and I went to a meeting with the government of the region of Loreto to discuss the conservation zone that they are planning for the Maijuna lands. Mike did a masterful job of lobbying and convinced them to significantly increase the size of the area designated as pristine and free from any extraction to include a rare hilly portion of the jungle that is near Totolla, the destination for the second half of our trip.

When Jake arrived I showed him around the city. People here seem intrigued and somewhat bemused by gringos but are very friendly. Some of the young guys seem to be into U.S. culture and say things like "What's up brother?" And the women seem to be intrigued by gringo men, particularly Jake, who is taller and younger than I. They do not approach us, but give very friendly glances. After lunch we met another friend of Mike's named Heroclides, Spanish for Hercules. These guys have the best names. So far I had met

Hercules, Elvis, Roosevelt, and Victor Hugo, and Sebastian's nickname is The Red Monkey.

***

The market of Belen is on top of the river bank, up from the slum of the same name. It is a massive swirl of vendors that takes up several blocks. The most common stands featured meat and fish, cut and butchered before our eyes, fruit, and herbal remedies. Everyone tried to sell us performance enhancing tonics and what was purported to be ayahuasca, a local hallucinogenic drug. The place was also filled with massive vultures that perched on the rooftops and wandered underfoot, picking up the butcher and fish scraps. They had absolutely no fear of the throngs of people, and a bold buzzard practically landed on my shoulder.

There were also rows of women rolling cigarettes from massive mounds of freshly chopped tobacco, sealing the papers with a gum made of yuca and grapefruit. We also saw caiman claws, python heads, skins of anaconda and a huge and highly venomous bushmaster snake, and the pelts of otters, jagaurundi, and a jaguar.

Just down the river bank is the expansive shanty town of Belen. It was the edge of Belen that I had seen on my morning run, but we now sought out a guide to take us into the heart of the impoverished village. We asked a few vendors to suggest a guide and suddenly a little fellow appeared and cheerfully announced: I am George, which I initially took as "I am yours." This guy had a haircut from an Ah Ha video and a letter of recommendation from the manager of the Ahwahnee Lodge in Yosemite. He insisted on speaking English and was filled with so much energy that we could not resist settling on him as our guide. At that time some young guy approached Jake, playing a wooden flute and offering to get high on weed or ayawasca. Somehow he ended up tagging along on the tour.

About a third of the way down the ancient, eroded steps to the river we crossed the high water mark of the recent flood. Beneath us the damage inflicted was immediately apparent. The slapdash corridors between the ramshackle houses were filled with muddy ridges of detritus: shoes, trash, furniture, bottles, human waste, everything that had washed up and settled onto this muddy flood plain turned city.

Every time someone greeted George, he proudly announced that everyone in Belen knew him. He took us deeper and deeper down the gentle slope towards the water. With each step the piles of muck got higher and the smell got more strangling. Finally the makeshift road turned into a canal, and we were limited to a narrow sidewalk along the houses. Cheerful old men drinking rum straight from their basement stills greeted us with boisterous shouts. At this point the houses were on stilts, but even the upper levels had been flooded. At the point where even the sidewalk reached the water there were several long handmade boats. George loaded us into one narrow and rocky boat and off we went through the fetid water. The canal through the village opened into the Itaya River. On what appeared to be the opposite bank were many more shanties. As we approached we saw that this was simply the floating extension of Belen.

George pointed out the highlights of the floating village, including schools and churches. We passed people bathing and washing clothes and dishes in the filthy water. George reached down, cupped his hand, and demonstrated that the residents drank this water. Of course, he told us how sick we would be if we did the same, but he had spent his life in Belen and his body was prepared for the barrage of microbes and pollutants.

Eventually he took us to his house. The raft of tree trunks that defined his domain measured perhaps five by eight meters. A roof covered the whole raft, but only a small portion had walls made of boards and blankets. In this area, perhaps the size of a king-sized bed, George lived with his wife and four children. He also had a small dog and four cats that wandered around the raft. His neighbors had a healthy flock of chickens.

The most striking thing about Belen is how cheerful and friendly the kids are. They have everything they need, that any of us need. Being greeted by so many of them changed my mindset entirely. I had entered Belen pitying their squalor but ended up pitying the rest of us who think that we need so much more than a roof, food, water, and supportive companions.

After the boatman, who was George's neighbor, took us back to the shore, George guided us back up to the market. We paid him ten Soles each, the equivalent of four dollars, which covered the tagalong flautist as well.

In the evening, Jake and I walked to local market and got some beer to drink poolside. We watched the bats and lizards flit about and talked about travel, music, and other shared interests. For dinner we went to one of the few fine restaurants in Iquitos. A motokaro took us to a well built porch over some stairs down to the river. Here we boarded a boat that seemed like the QEII compared to our afternoon craft. The boat took us maybe a kilometer out into the river to a floating restaurant. The two-story structure was made of beautifully polished wood and featured an enticing freshwater pool, lit blue in the dark night. Soft ambient music completed the scene. The food was spectacular, as was the view of the city, yet the total bill for beer, appetizers and entrees was under 200 Soles, or around 80 dollars. It was such a stark contrast to the afternoon poverty and a surreal way to end a long and adventurous day.

***

Jake and I started the morning with a 7:30 motokaro ride to the airport to meet the students, which was a blast because the rickety craft could accelerate to hair-raising speeds outside of town. We passed a protest at the Palace of Justice—which I assume is the equivalent of a state supreme court—that was closely watched by police in full riot gear. It was already sunny and sort of hot when we greeted the students at the airport. We all piled into two shuttle vans to the hotel and helped them get settled in.

The student group consists of four engineering students: Gabe, Rob, Jose, and Lawrence; Sara, a nursing student; Leslie, who takes international relations; and Laura, who studies public health. After the students showered and ate breakfast, we took half the students to get our rubber boots for the jungle. We will put those on when we get off the boat in Sucasari tomorrow and wear them until we return to Iquitos, except for when we sleep or swim. The other students went with Barry, the engineering professor, to get hardware for the bio-sand water filters.

We reconvened at lunch to discuss how we will explain hygiene to the people of Sucasari, some of whom do not really understand germs, hydration, and other facts that we take for granted, although our great grandparents did not understand them either. Because of this lack of understanding, many of their babies die of dysentery and other easily avoided or treated diseases. Sara devised a demonstration of the spread of germs using glitter, which stuck to lotion-coated hands but was passed from person to person through contact.

The highlight of the day so far was going to the home of the regional official in charge of conservation areas. He was the top dog at the meeting that Mike and I attended yesterday. After some back and forth in the motokaro, we found the street number next to an inauspicious open door. A man inside said that he would get the official's wife. The entrance was a garage containing two motorcycles next to a small courtyard. The courtyard had no roof but was protected from intruders by rebar.

Our hostess welcomed us into a massive grand parlor paneled in deep wood and furnished with plush armchairs and the two longest sofas I have ever seen, all antiques. In the next room, which was also enormous, were a large dining table and a massive and well-stocked bar made of the same wood as the paneling and ceiling. The hostess was quite a talker and told us many details about her life, including the fact that her young son Waldo, who came out to greet us, was born near my home town of Raleigh, NC. Because he is a U.S. citizen, she cannot get a visa to visit her sisters, who live in Miami and Texas, which struck me as highly perverse.

On the way back we came upon a parade celebrating the 159th anniversary of El Nino Jesus de Praga, a statue of Christ with a huge crown erected in Prague in the 17th Century. The parade kicked off with two guys on stilts, followed by large wagons filled with children. Each wagon had a theme that seemed to celebrate the miracle of Disney movie commercial tie-ins.

***

We made the most of our last night before heading to Sucari. We met the students for a brief meeting to set our plan for today and then returned to Kiki Riki, the rotisserie chicken place from the first night. We then returned to the floating bar and had an absolute blast. I discovered that they carried a Peruvian dark beer, which was delicious compared to most of the bland beer choices. They also had a dejay spinning even better music than the previous night. He was a nice English kid and a dead ringer for young Mick Jagger.

We met lots of other people there, including the owners and the guitarist for an all-female Swedish metal band and her Norwegian friend. In a city where anything goes, whether technically legal or not, this bar was like an offshore island with no rules. But everyone there was very chill and friendly. Between the music, the beer, the surreal location, and the friendly interesting people from around the world, it was really about as close to paradise as I could imagine.

The bar owners are a couple, both of whom speak very good English. She spent a decade in Los Angeles, and he claimed to go to Georgetown. But he also claimed that he grew up in Belen, that his father was a Fullbright scholar, and that he had dated two Miss Perus and the wife of George, our Belen guide. His wife claimed to have been an aspiring actress in Los Angeles but that and her other claims were all credible, unlike some of her husband's. Not all the pieces fit together, but they were great company.

Despite our late night, I was up and waiting for the people who said that they would meet me for a 6:30 run. The only hearty souls who joined me on the run were Sara and Leslie, who had left the bar earliest last night. Jake, Gabe, and Lawrence had all said they would come, but I knew that they were highly doubtful.

The three of us ran along the river to the market above Belen, probably a little over a mile away. We then sought out glitter in the market to use for a hygiene demonstration in Sucasari. It is amazing what you can get at 7:00 AM, but we failed in this mission, partly due to the fact that we have not been able to determine the Spanish word for glitter.

On our run back to the hotel a few people ran along next to us for short spurts. The kids and some adults here get a kick out of that, I guess because they see running as an oddity. The men who we passed seemed to enjoy the fact that my friends were running in sports bras and no shirts.

***

After waking up Jake and Jose, we assembled in the lobby and headed to the docks and the boat that will take us into the jungle. Jose and a local guy went to find glitter and meet us at the boat. We had to take several motokaro taxis to the docks and paid some guys a few soles to carry all of our stuff down the long steep stairway to the boat.

The boat was long and narrow, with ten rows of fours seats, two on either side of a center aisle. It had a canvas roof but was open on the sides. There was a shabby little restroom near the stern motors.

The boat was filled with Gerardo, Sebaco, Heraclides, the seven students, two crew members, Mike, Jake, and me. So we all got seats on the open sides of the boats and most of us had rows to ourselves.

After what seemed like endless delays, we finally shoved off and picked our way through the un-choreographed crowds of boats in the river. We were gone about ten minutes or so when I saw Heraclides talk to Mike and then to the boat captain. The captain sighed and whipped the boat around. Mike explained that they had forgotten the harnesses that Heraclides fashioned to climb the tall trunks of the aguaje palms to sustainably harvest the fruit.

The fruits fetched a good price in Iquitos and were for sale whole or in juice form by street venders all over the city. Traditionally the trees were felled to harvest the fruit, but they take decades to grow, so scaling the tree with a machete to remove just the fruit provides a means for the Maijuna to extract and sell their resources without depleting them. One of our missions in Sucasari was to teach the villagers to use the harnesses and to provide one per household.

We all waited on the boat while Heraclides taxied to his house to get the harnesses. After he returned we shoved off again and were finally on our way. As much as I loved Iquitos, I was most excited about getting out into the jungle and away from electricity, running water, machinery, and other signs of modern civilization.

PATRICIA WELLINGHAM-JONES

Emails to My Son

9/8/10 Here's a neighborhood-village memory I have but you were too young to remember. We 3 lived on Upper Stanyan in the Haight-Ashbury for several months while you were a baby, 1965-66, just before the big flower child invasion. It was an international village. Afternoons I'd wheel you in a stroller down the hill and along Haight, in and out of the shops, buying what I needed for dinner. The shoppers and storekeepers would chat, chuck you under the chin, give you a little treat, all very friendly and casual. There was also a local pub/bar where we'd congregate, not to get drunk but to visit with pals, stroller and all. Also connected to that: a black couple owned the big old house where we rented a flat and they adopted you/us, even had us to their home further down on Fell. They were unofficial grandparents to you for the few months we lived there. Hadn't thought of that for years..

5/6/13 Kentucky Derby Day: your Grandfather C (my dad) adored the horse races (despite being a most responsible banker) and went to several in our region (as far south as Baltimore etc.) as often as he could get there. One year he was invited by clients to the Kentucky Derby, nice hotel, special box at the races with the bigwigs, the whole works. He was in heaven. Had a fantastic time, the ultimate for a lover of the ponies. He had another memorable horse race event when he and his good pal went, as they so often did, and the other man keeled over with a heart attack right there at the races and died in Dad's arms. Horribly shocking, but a great way for him to go, doing what he loved, though pretty rough on my father. I too enjoy the races but hardly ever have a chance to go. Last year though M, J and I went on one of our day trips to Golden Gate Fields (or is it Bay Meadows? one is still here, one is gone) and had a fantastic time. The first time any of them had been to a real thoroughbred racetrack and their eyes were wide all day long.

5/10/13 Another Grandfather C story you'll enjoy, you with your socialist leanings. He was a lifelong Republican (NJ middle class, what else?) and though he and Mother scraped through the Depression, they emerged with very little and it was that way for a long time. Dad went to work for the National Bank of M when it was a small frame house; he was the dogsbody, did everything from man the furnace to shovel the snowy sidewalks to act as teller then later arrange loans. From that beginning he built a 50+ year career and wound up as president then chairman of the board of directors of a small chain of banks. All by way of saying that when Mother finally got her mink stole (lifetime dream for some reason) and could wear it to their bank parties/conventions/functions, she relished the role of Mrs. Banker. Dad, however, never could stand fools and idle chitchat and really disliked sniffing up to the wealthy so he would be found in a dark corner somewhere, sipping his Manhattan and deep in conversation about the horses etc. with the janitor, a man he much enjoyed. I've always kept that memory; when I was older and went with them I saw it myself. It surfaces in almost all social gatherings which I find brutally boring.

10/17/09: Dairyville Orchard Festival

Had a great time at the Orchard Festival after not going for a year or so. Huge crowd, Jenny and I had to park on the highway across from Lassen View School, which actually was closer than some of the parking areas. We first checked out the lunches, bought our tickets for the carnitas/beans/rice/tortilla one, then started making the rounds of all the booths: art, candles, soaps, crafts, clothes, etc. and food. Indeed yes, local food. We grazed our way through nuts (almonds, walnuts, pecans, pistachios), olive oils (lemon was best) with French bread cubes for dipping in that and balsamic vinegar (lots of different places, so more bread than I normally eat in a week), apples, prunes, the 36-Lady Prunecake (which we ordered as bundt and will divide), soup mixes, even jams (bought prickly pear jalapeno and tomato which are heavenly on crackers with cream cheese). Was tempted by a vest and by soy candles, held myself back. Wilted by heat and high humidity and 1.5 hours of walking, we picked up our lunches in to-go boxes and headed home for naps. Our Festival has gained momentum and every year sees more vendors, more attendees. Fun to see neighbors and people I don't usually see, to be part of the community again.

7/3/13 I have a bird story, just happened. Heard a fuss outside the door, looked out to see a jay harassing a barn owlet in the maple tree by the patio. He'd apparently tumbled from the nest and was trying to figure out what to do next. I grabbed the camera, sending the best of the lot I took. Baby jumped up then fluttered off but wasn't skilled enough to keep flying so hopped on the ground to the road then across where he found some small trees I fervently hope he's climbing little by little. He'd gotten up a few feet when I left; they have dogs and cats there and I hope nobody finds the little guy so he can survive. I love those owls, thrilled to see him so close, though wish he was safe inside his box or on a tree branch with his sibs, strengthening his wings. Time will tell and I'll probably never know what happens. Though I'll hear the sibs taking flight tonight, I bet.

4/25/15 To Alma and MN, Pat too: This morning I went to the biennial quilt show at the RB fairgrounds. Remember going with me about 6 years ago, Alma? You were with me in spirit today, snorting in disdain - not 'real' quilting - that only 6 of the 200 on display (not counting the booths and sales areas) were hand quilted. I enjoyed the artistic aspect of the quilts despite the machine quilting and think a good many of the quilt were done by hand.

The other thing that fascinated me about this particular show was the theme, The Secret Language of Quilts, and the excellent display showing various quilt patterns used in the Underground Railroad days of slaves escaping to freedom. These were handed down in oral histories of women through the generations though there is very little written about the subject. Patterns like bear paw meaning keep to the animal trails not roads, log cabin for safe place to rest, etc. There was also a display of various patterns related to messages hobos riding the rails left for one another, some similar, others signifying things like dog present or big man in the house. Only a few of the quilts on display actually were about this pair of themes, though, which was a bit disappointing. Anyway, it made for a lovely excursion topped off with a Wendy's chili-cheese potato which I brought home to enjoy with a book for a late lunch.

7/13/11: Yesterday neighbors appeared at my door saying Donnie killed a baby rattlesnake in his veggie garden on our property line. Uh oh. Wonder where mama and siblings are? Hope Patch the cat doesn't come across them, or worse, bring one inside. Life in the country, sigh... Later: Yeah, sure would hate to stub my toe on a rattler in the dark. That's a lovely thought. I'll think positive, and keep the hoe handy outdoors. That's how we killed them in the camp you remember from age 3-5 and I don't have a gun to shoot them, not that I'd manage to hit the head if I did. I do have my baseball bat by the bed and could always scream for a neighbor but that's not my style, much better to be prepared... You may not remember this story but one of those summer days at camp the counselors took the body (head buried) of a rattlesnake into the kitchen, dangling from their hands about 4 feet, and asked the city cook to fry it for them. She promptly passed out. As I spent a lot of time helping in the kitchen (I do love kitchens, you know) I blasted the girls, got the cook to bed, then reluctantly volunteered to cook the damn snake if they prepared it. Late that night, after the kids, and you, were asleep, I cooked snake disks and we ate them with Pepsi around the fire. Fun memory. Not that I'd like to repeat it. And yes, it did taste like chicken...

5/10/10 What a grand afternoon at Red Bluff's first ever Well-Being Faire. Lots of woo-woo stuff (tarot, palm reading, numerology, aromatherapy) but also massage and knitting lessons and health info booths. I was the poet of the event – read twice, at 2 and again at 3. Not many people but those who did listen really enjoyed it. What made it so special was 11-year-old Lisa, 6th grader at Lassen View. As I was laying out my books, she picked one up and softly sang the poem to herself. I asked if she'd like to sing a couple of them in the first reading and she loved the idea. So she picked 2 from Alyssum Asylum and 1 from Voices on the Land and, when we got started, I introduced her and she made up her music as she went along.I enjoyed it and the audience was receptive and warm. She gave me some hugs and darted off to find her mother, who had one of the booths. I told her she could come back at 3 and do it again if she wanted, and she did – with different poems this time. I gave her the 2 books as thanks and she was waving them around when I left.

4/7/11 I've enjoyed all my bus trips but this was the best, I think. We went to Crocker Art Museum in Old Town Sac'to; it's been renovated and expanded from the original 1800s mansion (a major thing of beauty all on its own). I esp liked the new ceramics exhibit from a man who unexpectedly got hooked on handmade vessels and wound up with a huge collection which he donated. After that we drove east into rolling foothills to Loomis (Roy lived there at one time and commuted to work in Sac'to down I-80) and High Hand Nursery and Cafe where we had a delicious lunch of asparagus ginger soup, turkey sandwich and salad. Then wandered through the plants, a small art gallery, an oriental rug shop. It's an old fruit packing shed brought back to life. Then we went east again, further up into the Gold Country out of Auburn to Rick and Janet Nicholson's 2 person glass blowing business. Fascinating, esp as I'm part of a NJ glass blowing family from the 1700s to 1982 when my father's cousin retired. They produced 3 pieces while we watched and asked questions; their work is all over the world in commissions, galleries, museums, all from this small parcel in the countryside where they also raised 2 daughters. Last stop of the day was at Bootleggers, a neat old restaurant in Old Town Auburn for dinner. Beamed rafters, old brick walls, stone fireplace out of a novel, etc. and most enjoyable. Got home at 9:15, very tired, but with great memories.

11/29/09 Today I scattered Phil's ashes. Weather was crisp and clear, trees were still clad in gold and copper and brown, and I turned the day into a trip down memory lane. First was breakfast in RB. I then went up outside M past where Roy had a cabin when the children were young and into the woods along Rock Creek, where Phil and Roy (and Roy and I) loved to fish and picnic; there I scattered Phil's remains, to soak back into the soil of the place he loved so much. Then I took the Forwards Mill loop around the top of M past the old abandoned sawmill (a skin of ice on the millpond) and down the other side, past places Roy and I walked and went to cut cedar firewood in the early days. Back through M and out over the Lanes Valley loop to Hwy 36 and so down into RB and home. Past a lot of places and things Roy and I enjoyed over many years of roaming our region. A very nice 100 mile memory-ride... Now I'm taking the rest of the day to be alone, no writing, no friends for tea. Just need all these memories and impressions to soak into me again...

7/10/11 Sherry A couple of days ago Jenny sent me an interesting article on sherry, which sparked the idea of having our own sherry tasting as she has some cream sherry and I have a CA medium dry. Today I went to RB to try to find a 'real' sherry, one from Jerez, Spain. Went first to CVS which didn't have any sherry at all, though I did get some brandy on sale. Over to Raleys, our quality market, and found just one pair from Jerez: a cream sherry and an amontillado, which is what I'd wanted. Picked up a bottle (a bit pricey, at that) and took it to the checkout. Woman checker: Are you cooking with that? Me, with horrified look: No, I'll sip it. Checker: You'll sip it when? Me: Before dinner, or after dinner – or in the middle of the day. We both laughed.

8/11/11 Jenny and I held our sherry tasting after 'The Closer' and before pizza. I got out the little dessert glasses Roy and I bought in an antique shop in Old Town Auburn, CA and the 3 sherry glasses from one on top of the wall surrounding the ancient town of Chester in England, added a pressed glass one from the early 1900s US; it was fun to use them again. We tasted a CA medium dry sherry along with an amontillado (medium dry) from Jerez, Spain. They matched in category. The CA sherry was mellower, lighter in color, with a nutty flavor; the true Spanish sherry was darker, a bit sharper in flavor and rich; both rather sweet. It was almost a tie, though we both edged a bit in favor of the CA. After dinner we had cantaloupe on the creek deck with the Spanish (from Jerez) cream sherry and it was so sweet it almost made my teeth grind. Very rich and dessert-like and a few sips were a pleasure, after that it got cloying (but I don't care much for sweets, so there's bias, I fear). An interesting and fun tasting and we both decided we'd like to keep sherry on hand, it's an elegant drink.

9/6/14 This morning I went to the annual Tehama Museum Jubilee. Roamed the vendors set up all around the park, bought some fresh prunes (Tehama Co. is the primary prune growers in the country and

I've been watching the harvest equipment rumble over the bridge and past the house for weeks). Anna Chrasta exhibited her art; local family but lives in SF as an artist, owns one of the big old Painted Ladies there, and I quite liked her work. A weaver was all set up at a big old floor loom and wove a rug of strips from T shirts her friends gave her in purple, blue, red, some sage green and sand thrown in for contrast. Fascinating and satisfying for a demonstration as it grows fast while still showing all the technique. I told her about MN Pat's class in Navajo weaving, how tedious and difficult it was and she wouldn't be doing another rug though glad she was doing it once. The weaver picked up the comb and showed me why it was such a task - each row tamped down by the inch manually. We agreed that different cultures had different weaving methods and styles according to place and life, most interesting. Some spinners were at work too. After that I went to the country store section and got 36 Ladies Prune cake, one for my freezer, one for Jenny. Then outdoors to buy a big slice of homemade rhubarb pie to go and had a hamburger/potato salad lunch (burgers flipped by Bill at the market who gave me free green beans yesterday) with a couple of women from out of town who were enjoying our small town festival. There was music, I left before the speeches.

7/20/11 We had a lot of excitement around here in the middle of the night. Not sure of details till I call Lon, the neighborhood snoop, but I think he or son-in-law Donnie or both chased an intruder (likely drug related, most crimes here are) who splashed across the creek and was found and subdued in the shrubs and blackberries by the cops. At least 2 sheriff's cars, lights flashing, sirens blasting, swooped down on us then a fire truck. When I realized it wasn't at my house, I went on the creek deck and watched from a safe distance till they took the guy(s) away.

Later: You'll be relieved at my further report on the night's alarms. Lon assured me he and Donnie were not involved at all, the action took place on the other side of the creek. Later in the day he checked the jail roster online (he does keep his nose to the wind) and it was a cousin of the troublemaker who grew up across the creek. Evidently cops chased him down 99 in a stolen car, he leaped out and away down the ancient road along the creek that very few know about, the cops chased him from that direction but, in a pincer movement, others arrived from the Sherwood (my road) direction and got him in the middle. Other charges were involved and bail is so high it'll probably not be met for the multi-time offender. We've got a lot like him in this area, poverty and drugs are rife, plus gangs are increasing. Troubling times. However, as a mystery reader, it was interesting to watch the action from the safety of my deck.

4/21/13 Yesterday's vaulting and wine tasting event was held in a huge barn plus arena just a few miles from home. Francia took me and her nephew Etienne so we could drink wine. She'd be our driver. The wines were from the monastery just down the road, and quite nice. The food was fantastic! Steamed asparagus wrapped in either Swiss cheese or ham thinly sliced (cream cheese was the 'glue'); a shrimp salsa; brie baked in a pie, either fig and onion or cranberry and walnut, both delish; olive oil from down the road drizzled over French bread; and cupcakes served with Port (I had seconds on a red wine and brie instead of the sweet). The vaulting was fun to watch and astounding to see these young people—and even a mom, Francia's daughter Maite—swing up on a huge draft/quarter horse and strike poses, even while trotting. Their balance was hard to believe and the strength those small girls had, plus flexibility. The goal of the fundraiser is to pay for the horse's way to their first national competition in Denver this summer and it was fun to watch them work on their group exercise. I'll give them another donation down the road to help them all get there.

4/9/14 Funny story from Monday morning's weekly jaunt to our little LM library. I'd checked out my books, then remembered I wanted to see if any of the sale books would work for this trip so I pulled one out of the cart – and ladies' panties fell at my feet. I said, "I know this is the local hub for social activity but isn't this a bit much?" Our young male librarian picked them up with a plastic bag over his hand (like doggy-do scooping), dropped them in the trash and hurried to wash his hands.

2/4/10 Marilyn's kitty had a stroke during the night, so she checked with the vet after the film and no, poor little thing wasn't going to make it. I went with her while she had Fredericka (Freddie) put down, then I carried the box of remains home while Charles dug the grave in the pet cemetery. We've all lost many pets, but that doesn't make it any easier, and we always grieve for the one that's gone. Glad I could be there to provide a hug for her, think it does make things a little bit better.

My girls are getting old too—Java 17, Smudge 13—but are enjoying their lives, as much as I can tell. Poor Java gums me to death with love, leaves little crescent snail tracks down my arm from her toothless mouth. Smudgie's only got 8 teeth left and they're at random so chewing must be interesting for her. J just gulps the kibble whole, then sometimes leaves piles of it on the white carpet, little greedy guts.

11/15/14 A woman I've known for years was directed to me by satisfied clients and managed to pull me 'out of retirement' as she put it to edit her memoir. So I've been doing that for the past week or so, and loving every minute. Just about to hand it back to her with 3 pages of suggestions that'll make her cringe but result in a much better book if she follows them. Plus, I'm getting $40 an hour, the going rate. She's lucky because I work fast so it won't be as much as it might have been, and we're both lucky because she's a skilled writer so that part of it doesn't need a whole lot of work. She does have major work ahead if she wants it to go public, however, as she was so busy with catharsis that much needs to be pruned out (it's boring!) for general reading. As always, the writer does what s/he wants. This is only the opinion of one person.

RAYMOND M. WONG

Words Unspoken

1-10-13

Dear Father,

Where to begin? The Chinese, that would be the place to start. I stopped speaking Cantonese shortly after arriving in America. It didn't take long to learn English; I watched TV.

Mom had married Roger, a Navy man from Minnesota. I was nine when we moved to China Lake, a naval base in the Mojave. Roger had a friend whose seven-year-old daughter, Wendy, always wanted me to play dolls or some such nonsense. I complained, but my mother told me to humor the girl. A lot older and more mature, I refused to play girly games.

Wendy once asked me to read a picture book to her. "Nope," I said. She brought the book to my mom, who tried to read to Wendy.

I scooted next to them on the couch to watch. My mother's English wasn't great and she skipped over words she didn't know. Whenever my mom missed a word, I pointed to it and said, "What about this one, Mom? What does that say?"

She ignored me.

After we returned home that night, my mother lit into me. How dare I humiliate her? I was a smart aleck and good for nothing. I was never to do anything like that again, did I hear her?

Mom always harped on me: I watched too much TV. I refused to speak Chinese. I didn't take out the trash. I slouched and spent too much time alone. I always sided with Roger.

And she didn't spare Roger: his drinking, smoking, ill temper, his crazy spending and utter disregard for her.

Did she do that to you, Father? Pinpoint your failings? Is that why she left you in Hong Kong? Did she ever tell you that?

1-11-13

Dear Father,

I found out about my friend's death yesterday. Paul was a literary agent who handled my memoir from 2006 to 2009. I met him through an editor at a newspaper.

Paul was in his late 80s and suffered from health problems: skin cancer and surgery on his knees, so he couldn't send out my manuscript for long stretches.

We became friends through our work. One summer, he invited me to bring the kids to a park near his condo. We met in front of his complex, and it took us a while to get to the park because Paul used a walker. He and I watched from a bench on the grass as Kevin and Kristie booted a football back and forth. In a gravelly voice uttered through wheezy breaths, Paul related that Kevin was an athlete; he could tell by the spring in the boy's step. I wondered how long it had been since this man had thrown or kicked a football.

I hung out with Paul that afternoon and remained his client in the ensuing years, prodding myself to be patient with his inactivity on my manuscript because he had liked my work enough to represent me. I owed him that much.

I eventually grew tired of waiting. In one of our last phone conversations, I hesitated for a long time before blurting out that I wanted to send my memoir to small publishers on my own. There was an unbearable silence before Paul said he understood in a voice so soft and muffled I could barely comprehend him.

The next day, I went to pick up my manuscript. That was the last time I saw him.

1-12-13

Dear Father,

That's the thing about death, the finality of it. I will never talk to Paul again, nor visit him with my children, never again experience his sharp and engaging wit, the one he no doubt used to establish relationships with people, with editors, with me.

I feel guilty that I ended our professional relationship. I knew it was going to be difficult for him to realize he could no longer be my agent, no longer be my friend.

The hardest part about death is the finality of it.

I remember the day I got the call. My mom's voice, urgent, a tone of distress I had never heard before: "Ray, bad news. I talk to your uncle. Your father die."

I stood in the family room with the phone in my hand. I just stood there, unable to say a word. Finally, I managed to utter, "We'll talk later," and hung up.

1-12-13

Dear Father,

That's the thing about death.

I'm not going to see you again, and Kevin and Kristie will never meet you.

I know it was important for you to see them. Mom told me you had urged us to bring the children to Hong Kong. She said you wanted to see them before you died. Yes, she told me, but I didn't listen. I didn't act fast enough.

The thing you have to know is that we had planned the trip the year before you died. My mother informed Uncle Chun-Kwok. But we had a roof leak. It was an expensive fix, and we couldn't afford to repair the roof and fly the family to Hong Kong. So we cancelled the trip.

How did you feel when you found out we weren't coming? Did you think we didn't care?

It wasn't that. We were going to come. I swear it.

1-12-13

Dear Father,

Why couldn't you come to San Diego? That's the question that sears at me. The thing that keeps me awake in the pitch of darkness. Why was it so hard to get on an airplane to see your grandchildren?

And if you couldn't do that, did it really matter to you?

How important could I have been if you never contacted me for nearly three decades? You never visited. You never called. You never wrote a letter. I didn't know who the hell you were.

That's why I didn't bring Kevin and Kristie to Hong Kong. I

didn't know we really mattered to you.

I didn't know I mattered to you. What else am I supposed to think if you never contact me? What am I supposed to think?

1-14-13

Dear Father,

I'm sorry I didn't write yesterday. The alarm went off at 5:00, just as it does every morning, the clock I set a half hour early so it reads 5:00 when it's really 4:30, a sound machine that breaks into ocean waves cascading against the shore.

When I heard the ocean yesterday, I turned off the sound and held Quyen. I counted to ten to give myself a little more time before waking to write. Yesterday, I counted to ten three times and didn't let go of my wife. I wanted to feel her in my arms, my legs twining with hers, a gentle tangle of snaking limbs like ripe vines in a garden.

I wanted to stay with Quyen. It was Sunday, the kids didn't have to be in school, and Quyen didn't have to work until 10:00. I wanted to snuggle.

I held my wife, listened to her breathing, felt her legs wrapped between mine, her torso pressed to me, my face so close to her supple neck, her scent, the fragrance of soap, her hair, the long silky strands caressing my cheeks, delicate like Kristie's fingertips when she was a baby, a light touch upon my face, exploring the contours as if she had never felt anything so wondrous, so mysterious, so soft and warm.

I didn't get up, Father, and I didn't write to you. I'm sorry about that. I hope you'll forgive me, just as I hope you'll forgive me for not bringing Kevin and Kristie to Hong Kong.

It wasn't the money. That wasn't why we cancelled the trip. We could've managed it. That's the God's honest truth. We could've managed it, but we didn't. I didn't.

Can you forgive me?

1-15-13

Dear Father,

Kristie was scared last night and asked me to spend time with her. I told her I would, but lost track of time at the computer.

Kristie called from the bedroom ten minutes later: "Daja!" She and Kevin started using the term a few months ago.

I went into her room, and Kristie asked for a bedtime story. I sang a short lullaby instead.

Minutes later, I heard, "Daja!"

I walked back to Kristie's room. She pointed at the pink canopy above her bed and said, "It keeps moving, Daja."

I could make out the faint shadow of a birthday balloon atop her canopy.

Kristie said, "Daja, it's a ghost."

I nodded and went to get a stepstool. After I took the balloon out of Kristie's room, I went back to the computer.

A couple minutes later, I heard "Daja" again. Back to Kristie's room. My daughter peered at me from under her Tinker Bell blanket and said, "I'm scared, Daja. I read a scary story today."

I took a deep breath and leaned to kiss her forehead. I said, "Then try not to read scary stories, okay?"

"I know, Daja."

I went back out to the computer.

Later, when I entered my bedroom, Kristie was under the comforter, a look of mischievous satisfaction on her face. Quyen fluffed Kristie's pillow and put it under our daughter's head.

I turned to my wife, who said, "Kristie's scared, so she's going to sleep here tonight."

"What about you?"

"I'll sleep with Kevin."

I glared at Kristie, but the smug expression on her face told me the issue had already been decided. I took a deep breath, released it with an even deeper sigh, and went to brush my teeth before settling next to my daughter.

1-16-13

Dear Father,

I wish you could've been at Kristie's birthday. We invited five of her friends to the movies. The theater set up a table in the lobby and sectioned it off with life-sized character props.

We ordered cheese pizza, cake, and soda. The theater put "Happy Birthday, Kristie!" on the marquee, and she was so excited to see her name on a billboard.

We ate and sang Happy Birthday to Kristie. The girls, all studying Chinese at the same school, sang again in Mandarin.

Kristie opened gifts. Then the girls played video games in the lobby before our host took the entire group upstairs to tour the projection room. As the birthday girl, Kristie started the projector of her own birthday movie!

I wish you could've been there. Kristie would've introduced you to her friends. They would've spoken to you in Mandarin. I can picture Kristie talking to you. She would make you feel comfortable; she has that way with people. Quyen and I marvel at Kristie, because at the age of nine, she knows how to win people's trust.

Kristie loves to read Harry Potter and she adores animals. She would ask us to take you to the San Diego Zoo, so you could see Elephant Odyssey. She would convey all kinds of interesting facts about the variety of animals on our planet. She would tell you how much she wants a golden retriever and vent her frustration that her parents won't let her get one until she's sixteen. She would show you how mature and responsible she is right now.

Would you side with her, Father? She can be very persuasive. What would you say to your precocious granddaughter?

1-17-13

Dear Father,

What happened on the day my mother and I left Hong Kong? What was going through your mind?

Did you see us off to the airport? Watch from the terminal as our plane lifted into the air? Did you feel as if something precious was being taken from you?

I can only imagine what it would feel like to have Quyen leave with Kevin and Kristie. It would devastate me. I would lose it.

How did you deal with that? The woman you loved, the child you brought into the world, your wife and your son, going away, perhaps never to return.

Did you feel abandoned, alone, as if someone had ripped your insides apart? Yet you were still alive to feel every excruciating moment? Did you stand there for the longest time after the plane disappeared? Did your legs feel cemented into the ground? Did you stare into an empty sky with a cold ache in the middle of your soul?

How long did you stay there, Father? Minutes? Hours? Standing. Waiting. Hoping. For what? A chance that the plane would turn around? That it would come back and land and we would get off like passengers returning from a vacation? That my mom would come to her senses and realize we belonged with you?

Is that what you've always believed? Is that why you never came to see me in America? Why you never called or wrote me a letter?

America never existed for you, did it? You always thought we were coming back. And you waited and waited.

1-18-13

Dear Father,

I remember my first date with Quyen. We went to see "The Rock" starring Sean Connery and Nicholas Cage, because she liked action movies. We ate at a Coco's and talked about her life in Vietnam, her family, and past relationships. With an unwavering gaze, she told me she didn't like dishonest guys. She would only go out with one person at a time, and she expected the same from me. Being with her felt right.

What was it like when you met my mom in China? Did her smile make you giddy? Did you notice her eyes, the texture of her hair, the way she walked, her outgoing manner?

What did you talk about? What did you do together?

I heard you met her again years later in Hong Kong. How did that come about? Did you know you would marry her? Was there any clue that she would have a yearning for something more, something you couldn't provide?

After my mother took me away, why didn't you ever remarry? I came back to Hong Kong almost thirty years later. In that span, you must've known we weren't coming back, yet you remained single, alone.

Did you love my mom that much? Did you see marriage as a lifetime commitment never to be broken? Even if the woman you loved abandoned you?

Did you believe, with every fiber of your being, that your wife and son were coming back? Did you really believe that?

1-19-13

Dear Father,

I sometimes wonder what we would have done together if I had remained in Hong Kong. I have a memory of you resting on your back, your arm draped over your forehead as if to shield your eyes from the sun's glare.

That's the image I have of you. Not a word of kindness to comfort me when I was stressed, not the supportive touch of your hand on my shoulder, nor a soothing expression in your eyes in a moment of crisis. I cannot remember any other thing about you from the first five years of my life.

If my mother and I had remained in Hong Kong, would you have taken me to Victoria Peak? And what if I was reluctant to join the other kids? Would you have nudged me forward to the monkey bars? Or would you have led me to the telescope so I could gaze at the ships dotting the horizon like tiny toy vessels? Would you have ushered me to the concession stand to buy a double dip vanilla swirl ice cream served on a waffle cone in a snug white napkin?

Would we have talked or would it have been enough to just spend time in each other's company?

Would you have guided me throughout the playground, hand in hand, while I gawked in silence at the other kids? You would've let me observe them. You would've accepted that as part of my nature, a boy wandering without aim surrounded by high-pitched screams and boisterous, bubbling laughter, and you would've been content to be with me, a boy you loved and treasured more than anything on this precious planet.

You wouldn't have told me this, but I would have known. I would have known.

3-25-13

Dear Father,

Kevin celebrated his twelfth birthday by inviting three of his best friends over to play Beyblades, a game of spinning battle tops launched into a plastic stadium. In the morning, Kevin couldn't wait for the party to begin. He ran around the house, jumped onto the seat of my office chair, and terrorized Kristie so much she complained about him.

When his friends came over, Kevin engaged in Beyblade battles in the living room. Then our family took the group to Peter Piper Pizza for lunch and arcade games. Kevin enjoyed being with his buddies throughout the day, but after his friends left, Kevin discovered two of his Beyblades missing. He checked everywhere and could not find them. Quyen suggested one of his friends might have accidentally packed them away with the toys they had brought over.

Kevin was subdued and the excited glint had vanished from his eyes. He went into his room and closed the door. Kevin stayed there a long time, and though I wanted to go in to comfort him, I needed to respect his privacy.

Later that evening, Kevin came out of his room with a phone in his hand and a brightened expression on his face. He announced to the family in a tone of unbridled enthusiasm that a friend had found the Beyblades in a backpack mixed in with the other toys he had brought to our house. Kevin said, "Now I don't have to worry about them anymore."

I went to Kevin and hugged him. Quyen said, "Kevin, the Beyblades aren't the important thing. The trust in your friends is something that means so much more."

Kevin said, "Yeah, that's why I called my friends. I had to know."

4-28-13

Dear Father,

My family grieved at your funeral. Quyen, Kevin, Kristie, and even my mother cried at the sight of your lifeless body on the metal platform. I couldn't cry. I put on the face of the dutiful son, wore it like the white canvas smock I had on over my clothes. White, the color of mourning in Hong Kong, the headband made of the same coarse material, the ritualized clothing everyone in my immediate family donned to commemorate your passing.

It felt like a play, and I was a costumed character trying to figure out my lines. I watched, cold and detached, as Kevin and Kristie dropped paper money into the furnace outside of the viewing room, a wish for you to have all that you needed in the afterlife.

I was in my head when the priest led us through the funeral hall, when he placed a coin inside your mouth to symbolize wealth and good fortune for your children after your death. In this case, it was one child, a son who couldn't even speak your language.

I walked behind the priest and listened to his rhythmic Chinese chant, his song of sorrow to honor your life as we proceeded to your cremation.

I didn't shed any tears then, but my family did. Kevin, Kristie, Quyen, and my mom. They grieved your loss.

Kevin and Kristie, the grandchildren you had never met. They cried when they saw you. They cried at the ceremony. They cried at your cremation.

I want you to know that. They knew you enough to cry.

The steel doors closed, and a conveyer pulled your coffin forward to the fire.

ANN SONZ MATRANGA

To Razela

Grandmother, did you leave with your hopes high? Did you look at your daughter, too sick to travel, and try to memorize her features, praying that you'd see her again before long?

Did you let yourself ask, how long?

Were you wearing a scarf and a long wool coat, bundled up, and were you cold?

Did you make the four children who went with you join hands, afraid you'd lose them in the crowd? Did you think you had a choice to stay or go?

Did you waiver?

Did you watch from the deck as the ship pulled away, until your sister and your daughter were just a speck on the dock? Was there a single moment when you held onto the rail to keep from jumping? Were you sick in steerage?

Did you cry?

When your ship approached the harbor, did you see the Statue of Liberty and did you believe the woman with the torch stood for good things to come? Did you wonder whether your husband would be waiting, and what did you think you'd do if you couldn't find him?

Were you scared?

Did you turn your face when a photographer took your picture or did you stare straight at him and hold your breath, pretending that he thought you were beautiful?

Were you angry?

Did you give your name in Yiddish to an English-speaking man and watch him write it down in unfamiliar letters that could have meant anything at all?

Did you care?

When you arrived on the mainland with your children and your bags, and walked to where families were waiting for their relations, how did you feel?

Were you proud?

If you had known from the start that it would all end for you in loss, and your children would grow up without you and your name would be forgotten, would you still have come here?

A FACE IN THE MIRROR

She entered the convent, bringing nothing with her from her former life but her old cotton underpants. All the rest was new. Her hair was cut short, almost buzzed. Over it she placed a stiff white shell called a wimple. It crossed her forehead, pulled so tight that it left a mark. Above the wimple she affixed a black veil made from thin cotton ironed perfectly to show no wrinkles. It fell to her shoulders like her lost hair and shifted back and forth as she walked. Around her neck she put a collar of starched cloth, white like the wimple, forming an oval that stopped just above her breasts, her poor unnoticed breasts, bound tight by a large bra with straps as thick as the shoulders of an apron, utilitarian, industrial strength. Over the white starched collar went the black habit, a shapeless dress with long sleeves, wide at the wrist, the skirt falling to mid-calf. Her legs stuck out below like dark poles in cement pilings, heavy shoes with laces threaded through holes that marched up her foot to her ankle. She was covered, crossed and veiled, and when she looked in the mirror it was as though she, Anna, had become invisible, except for her huge dark eyes, set too close, and her fine strong nose. These features made for a face that was out of place in nun's garb. It was a face from an Ellis Island photograph. It was a face from the lower east side, a woman at the market, a woman picking up her son from Yeshiva. It was a visible face, one that stood right out, not a Catholic face in a habit in the mirror.

THE DEAD AND GONE

When I was ten, I ran away to New York City to become an actress. I went to Broadway, where I imagined that I would meet producers who would give me a place on the stage. It didn't occur to me, or the policeman who lectured me when I got caught, that I was looking for the play I belonged in, the one with a leading role for a Jewish girl.

The part I was playing in real life was that of a girl from a Catholic family. Small and dark with close set eyes and a prominent nose, always absorbed in books and dreams, I stood apart from my tall, blonde, athletic companions. I watched them carefully to detect how to be like them, and prayed to Jesus to give me Irish dimples. Jesus became one of my imaginary friends.

When I was ten, an optometrist came to school to give eye examinations. I pretended that I couldn't read the letters on the wall because I wanted glasses. He tried lens after lens, and when none of them worked he concluded that I was lying. I felt that wearing glasses was a way to let others know that I didn't see them and they didn't see me, not really. I didn't even see myself.

In middle age I began to look for traces of my family story. I found a Polish Jewish pawnbroker grandfather who identified the white murderer of a black boy in East St. Louis in 1917, and it didn't make him popular. He went to prison for transporting guns across state lines, and later got rich in Miami. I found a grandmother who came from Poland, gave birth to my father and died three months later. She was only thirty-three. Her story and even her family name in Poland were forgotten.

I am the deputy of the dead and gone, the dishonored, the ones who vanished without a trace. I am not a knowledgeable deputy but I'm learning what I can, and even if I have to make up half of it as I go along, I'm the only one left standing who wants to tell the story.

BEING ME

I walked my dog Phinney uphill to the dog park. It was early Sunday morning, August, clear sky over the Bay, no fog. Inside the park I could let her off the leash as long as I scooped the poop. A dog-loving park neighbor had kindly tucked a pooper-scooper into a little nook for our use, and there was a stash of baggies too. A couple of men stood together talking. I overheard a few words. "Terrible… Can't believe she's dead…How did it happen?… Such a beautiful young woman… Troubled."

The dogs were racing around, yapping and making false growls.

Phinney, a beautiful dog with thick white fur, went over to the men. One of them leaned down to pat her and his dog rushed up to intercept the gesture. Phinney growled. I ran to put her back on the leash before there was an altercation. I wanted to inquire about the overheard conversation but I thought it might be intrusive. Too New York.

"You're so New York," my friend Anna told me. She was native Californian. "You ask questions I would never." She meant this in an admiring way, mixed with discomfort. I felt as though she could go either way with me, wanting to be more like me and yet embarrassed by me. I didn't want to be more like her, a triumph of age after many attempts to turn myself into a quiet-voiced, un-intrusive, keep-it-down kind of person. But in the park that morning I said nothing.

I walked Phinney back down the hill to the newsstand. The morning paper had just arrived with news of the death Princess Diana, a self-conscious, courageous, mixed up young woman who may have wanted to keep her mouth shut but she didn't know how.

GONE MOM

I entered Marywood Academy, a Catholic prep school for girls, in my junior year of high school, 1959. I had all the equipment and clothing on the list, the navy blue uniform, the heavy, laced shoes, the helmet for horseback riding, my nametags sewn into my undies.

I wasn't on the main corridor but off to the side, in a small, poorly lit room with an old wooden desk. The last, yellowed layer of varnish on the desk was peeling.

My roommate was a new girl too and I could see that we were different from the others, 'the old girls' as they were known, in a bad way. I wanted to get away from her, as though doubling the difference would make it hopeless.

My parents came with me to help set up my room. My mother was as different as I was, with her flowered hat and prominent nose. She was too small, too dark, and I felt endangered by her.

My mother was an artist and an art teacher. She knew things I would give anything to know now. But on my first day of boarding school, I was ashamed of my Jewish mother. Why the hell did she take me there?

SILVER BIRD

She was standing in the glass shelter at the trolley station looking down the track, her eyes narrowed to slits. With intense focus, she willed the train to come. The snow picked up, wind whipping light flakes into weapons that stung our faces. She wound her woolen scarf over her head and across her nose and mouth like a chador, leaving her dark eyes free. She seemed big to me, standing next to her, holding her gloved hand with my small one, my fingers clenched around hers like a vise. I felt like an anchor that wasn't quite strong enough to keep its boat from drifting out to sea. Her breath was thick as a storm cloud, cutting a wider swath than my small puffs.

She raised her free hand and her brow folded in a deep frown. I held my breath and my calves turned to stone, unable to move. She slammed her hand hard against the side of the shelter.

"Why is that damned train always late?" she said. "Mom," I whispered, "Please." I said it very quietly. Her face was angry, like a mean elf in a fairy tale, but her hand was warm around mine as though to protect me against the other hand, the angry one.

People sitting in the shelter glanced at us cautiously, and turned back to their newspapers. A woman close to us took a step further away.

I heard the sound of the trolley.

"Here it comes, Mom," I said.

"It's about time." She exhaled. Her grip relaxed. The lines on her face disappeared. She looked down at me with a small smile, let go of my hand and put her arm around my shoulder. Her wrist carried the scent of Chanel.

"Sorry Nancy," she said, "My feet are like blocks of ice."

Her silver bird earrings caught the light and sparkled. A man spoke to her when we were on the train. My mother, holding onto the overhead handle, leaned toward him. She smiled and my heart lit up like my flickering night light that sometimes worked and sometimes sputtered. I was like that light, plugged into my mother's unsteady current.

STOPPING TIME

July 4th, 1959. The night had grown dark and we heard the

rumbling sound of firecrackers. One after another, umbrellas of sparks lit up the horizon and showered down on the water.

"Here's to independence, Froggy," said Margarita, lifting a cup filled with beer. We were eighteen, just out of high school, and it was still a kick to be legal to drink. Frog was a nickname I gave myself in our freshman year at Marywood Academy when kids teased that I had green skin. It was their way of pointing out that they were fair and I was dark, and this was not a compliment. However, I laughed when I became Frog, and with that I owned the joke. I won.

As the evening came to a close we waited for the grand finale, a pyrotechnics display intricately mounted on a rectangular wooden frame. The band struck up The Star Spangled Banner, and red, white and blue stripes and brilliant white stars appeared against the black backdrop of the sky. The American flag shimmered for a moment in the hot, still air and burned out before our eyes in the late 1950s.

TINY DANCER

My mother lost the ability to walk after a single dose of chemo knocked her flat.

"The doctor said it's just a shadow," she explained, dismissing the significance of the mark on her liver. To find that mark she went through a scanning machine in a cold, fluorescent-lit room. At the far side of the room behind a glass wall, a man sat at a screen. While my mother shivered, a pasty nurse with pursed lips tried to inject her with something that would light up her insides.

On the third try I said, "That's enough. You have to stop." I was holding my mother's shaking hand.

"She has bad veins," the nurse said to the man watching the screen. He frowned and shook his head. "Okay," he said after a moment's pause. We've got enough."

My mother made a novena to St. Jude, the patron saint of lost causes, and she put an ad in the paper to seek St. Jude's help. She didn't tell me about this. I found the newspaper clipping in her wallet after she died. My father and mother started out as Jews and converted to Catholic. My father called a Rabbi friend in New York and asked him to pray for my mother. Between St. Jude and the Rabbi, he believed she would recover. My mother said, "Your grandmother lived to ninety-six. Eighty-four is much too young to die."

When mother couldn't walk anymore, she said she dreamed of dancing. My disabled brother walked her across the floor, each of them infirm, determined to make it, like fragile dance partners in a music box winding down.

RUN ALL THE WAY

I ran all the way to the hospital. It was a mile from my house. I didn't take the car because it was afternoon rush hour and I was sure it would take longer to drive than run, and I'd never find a place to park. I ran along the route that I often walked to work, down neighborhood streets, across a stream where the trolley tracks paralleled the water, over a small bridge with brick pillars, across a busy four-lane street ignoring the traffic light and the cross walk, and into the medical area. I ran at a steady pace, not fast, not slow, straight to the emergency entrance.

I introduced myself to the receptionist at the desk. "You called about my son? He was hit by a car?"

"We've been trying to reach you for an hour. Your son is here in the ER."

I sent my ten-year-old son off to school that morning in high water blue jeans with his sneakers tied tight and a corduroy zip-up jacket over his tee shirt. He had his lunch in a square red metal box, with a thermos full of milk, a tuna sandwich and two oatmeal cookies. I watched him from the kitchen window as he walked across the street. It was spring in Boston. The forsythia outside the window was in bloom and my view of him was framed in yellow. He had his homework in a red and blue vinyl case with a picture of Superman. He turned to wave at me before he crossed the street. He couldn't see me but he knew I'd be at the kitchen window.

"Where's my son?" I asked the ER receptionist. I was very calm. I spoke in a level voice and my hands didn't shake. My son was somewhere inside a door that she guarded, and I wanted to be admitted right away.

In one corner of the waiting room, two people sat side by side. The man had his arm around the woman. He was looking straight ahead. She clasped her hands together, staring down at them in her lap as though they held the answer to a question of life and death.

OUR UNEXPECTED LIGHT

The Christmas after 9/11, Grandma Jean gave me the book *An Unexpected Light: Travels in Afghanistan*. We were emailing back and forth about our wish to learn, to know something, to understand our suddenly changed relationship to a country we could hardly even place on the map. Jason Elliot, a young British man, traveled in Afghanistan as an apolitical observer in the late nineties and he wrote a luminous, literally light filled account of what he saw and heard there. I read this book with an ear for his prose and a pen in hand, underlining, trying to make it easier to track back to the facts that could guide me through current events.

Grandma Jean, the giver of this book, is not my grandma, but my daughter's grandmother by birth. She is my adopted daughter's deceased birth mother's mother. In a time of trouble in my daughter's life, we found her surviving birth family members and among them was Grandma Jean. When I read the book she sent me, I felt love from the woman who wanted to shed light on her daughter's reasons for giving up my daughter, whom she loved. Maybe this is a sign that the world can heal when broken hearts, broken promises and broken families fall under an unexpected light.

MY MOTHER'S EYES

"I'm Irish and African," I said to a neighbor outside my mother's house in Berkeley the week after she died. He had asked me whether I looked like my father. It was a backhanded way of asking, 'How come you don't look like your mother?'

He frowned and shook his head. "I thought your mother was Jewish."

"I'm adopted," I said. "My birth mother was on the Olympic ski team and my birth father is a jazz musician in New Orleans."

My imagination raced along the trails my birth parents might have followed. 'I'm going manic,' I thought. Making up stories felt like racing down a black diamond, almost out of control.

The guy's eyes darted away. "Well, your mother, she was a good neighbor," he mumbled.

'Most adopted children have fantasies about their birth parents,' according to a book I read in high school. I didn't have a conscious fantasy at the time. My emotional river flowed straight to my mother.

It was April, and purple blooms on jacaranda trees formed a canopy over the street. I got messages from friends in Aspen, where I had been working as a snowboard instructor. The snow pack was dissolving into the Roaring Fork and they were heading to the slopes in Chile, or finding summer work in the valley.

I had an unfamiliar, optimistic feeling when I opened the envelope from the adoption agency. Perhaps there would be a map to lead me to my other tribe, the one I resembled. In a dream I sat beside my mother with the letter open on a table between us. Her brown eyes were intent upon the words and her lips moved silently as she read it.

Finally she turned and looked straight at me. "Lindy," she said, "this letter is full of good news about you."

NANCY CANYON

After Twenty Years

5-14-2006

I'm sitting in bed on Monday morning, the morning after Mother's Day. Keri is pregnant. Bruce is saying he wants this relationship—this after telling me we are through because he is bi-sexual.

Now that I'm finished with school, I don't know what to do in regards to my next step with him. I'd like to feel more at home here in Bellingham, to get a job, to have a sense of being in the center of my life. I'm thinking it is time to close the book on my marriage. To say no to his cheating, even though he wants to preserve what is left of us.

I drew the Crow card this morning. It says, "As you learn to allow your personal integrity to be your guide, your sense of feeling alone will vanish. Your personal will can then emerge, so that you will stand in your truth. The prim path of true Crow people says to be mindful of your opinions and actions. Be willing to walk your talk, speak your truth, know your life's mission, and balance past, present, and future in the now. Shape shift that old reality and become your future self. Allow the bending of physical laws to aid in creating the shape shifted world of peace."

The part I like best about this: "As you learn to allow your personal integrity to be your guide, your sense of feeling alone will vanish."

5-15-06

I've been overdoing it lately—going to Kingston to work, fighting with Bruce—then driving home again. I know I want the money, but

140

can't I drum up three people to work on weekly here in Bellingham. That's $180/week. That would help out immensely. Things immediately necessary to deal with are:

1.   Defaulting to work like I did for Dad all those years. Quickbooks: I could take that class and learn it more in-depth so I could get a part-time job in an office. It's not bad doing money/writing checks, etc. I think most people get $15/hour for that type of job. Or I could finish filling out the second application for the bookstore. They seem to have a lot of fun over there.

2.   What to do with my stuff? The space I need to move things to Bellingham is much larger than the tiny little houses that cost 200,000 and up. What a difference from the nice house I got when I left Jack--$40,000. For a 2 bedroom. I could move back to Spokane, but then I wouldn't get to be around my future grandchild.

3.   Loneliness! When I think of a house, I think of sitting in it all alone. Being here in Fairhaven is active. Perhaps I'll proceed with the plan to check out the studio rental and try to get on at the bookstore. Those things sound easiest. My stuff can stay for now in our home, or I could go through it and have a sale. Put the antiques on consignment in a booth at a local antique store. Do I have enough stuff? Probably not. Price them and sell them. Or put them in storage until I have a house.

5-16-06

May will be over in not time. Last night I dreamt I was with a man whom I loved. It was that rosy, full hearted feeling of love. He hadn't been around in awhile and showed up with his wife. And there was something about them not being together for much longer that I seemed to know. I said to him, maybe we'll be together some day. That reminds me of what I said to Dr. M once. That was stupid of me/ he dismissed me from therapy shortly after that. He said he was attracted to me. I couldn't handle it, but tried. Then I turned giddy, thinking about him all the time. I hadn't thought of him in that way before he'd said that. I hate it still that I said I could feel the energy between us. It was weird. I wasn't doing anything that I knew I was doing. He seemed so vulnerable, so honest. Maybe I'll write him a letter. It is time to get rid of Bruce, after all. It is time to collect my belongings and put them all in one place—in Bellingham.

5-17-06

I'm having trouble with expecting participation in my life with others. I don't want to force myself on people, but what do you do to make friends? Get invited places, etc. It's been harder lately for me since I'm through with the main push of this school year. One more year, interesting. I'll get where I'm going—once I'm there I'll see if it's what I want or not. I liked the quote from the meeting, "We want the spring to come and the winter to pass. We want whoever to call or not call, a letter, a kiss—we want more and more and then more of it. But there are moments, walking, when I catch a glimpse of myself in the window glass, say, the window of the corner video store, and I'm gripped by a cherishing so deep for my own blowing hair, chapped face, and unbuttoned coat that I'm speechless: I am living...: Marie Howe, "What the Living Do."

So why do I have so much trouble living? I feel very dangerous lately—like things will implode or explode if I don't slow down. Even driving seems too reactionary—too chaotic. I forgot I was going to go to that reading at 7 PM tomorrow. Maybe I should email and tell her I forgot that plan, here I am back at my lovely indecision. It's easy to appreciate my creativity—not as easy to appreciate my sadness—or my neediness. I'm sorry if I'm needy—no I'm not sorry to be needed—I want to be needed—that's it, isn't it? I want to be needed—perhaps I can just believe I am needed. Boy I need a therapist big time...

5-18-06

When You Need Me
This is a friend
Holding my hand
Sitting with my mother
The whole family visits
And she brings a cake, Betty Crocker,
Iced with coconut and brown sugar
Sweet treat for visitors,
Sitting in close groups,
Handing out tissues,
One gone and the whole is partial,
And I went out to see
If her dog was in the car

A collie mix, a friend
I could see from the stoop,
Water running in the garden
Wind coming off the water,
I remember her gathering
Us together, feeding us,
We played all night
Because of her.

5-19-06

My life is now finding things to do, hopefully something that my heart wants to keep doing. What has fun and meaning? Not much right now—fun and meaning, that is. What to do about it? Get a pet. Where could I put a cat box? Is it time to look into finding a house in Bellingham or is this the wrong place for me to live? I could go to Kingston and stay awhile: garden, cook, try to work things out. I don't have a yard. I didn't know how much that would bother me. So what I need right now is more space to do art and a yard to garden in. Friendships and money. Four things not necessarily in this order. Money, friends, earth, and art. How could I get those all together? I don't like being so fixated on this problem. I don't like being a problem to Keri. Start looking for jobs, maybe it isn't working here because it isn't a good fit. Why would I go back if I have to worry about B cheating on me—even if he didn't actually go out with anyone?

5-20-06

Ah, the volcano exploded, when was that 70? There'll be a lot on TV about it today. I'll see if Debbie can get my Website updated, and then I need to learn to take care of it. Now things are settling out after that last full moon. I sort of went crazy with my last school mailing and all—over doing. I turned hyper.... But what I want now is to learn to not stand behind someone—and to know that it's okay for me to do what I love. And to have things that I want. Interesting how I've hoarded—I've thought I could only have what I took good care of. I think that is tied into base fear. Keep all my things because I won't get anything else. I just wanted toast. Bread is bad for me, and the effects last nearly a week. I just pulled the Rabbit Card. It says: Rabbit draws her fears to her by thinking about them. If there is a problem, let it go. Write them down and give them to the earth. Then write down what you want."

Maybe this could be a ritual I could do each day with smudge and a rattle. Know I am safe and free. I was in the triangle and didn't realize it. I went crazy instead.

5-21-06

Poem:

Days pass like liquid
My friends stopping,
Bringing their thoughts
And sweet energy.
I live in a house
in a neighborhood
Next door, an old woman
rocks, on the other side
a young family, it's
community I crave most.
The regularity of coming
together, eating potatoes
and coleslaw, sipping ice tea,
bowls of strawberries.
There is power in the group,
a helping hand offering the
resource of skill—
I am one with them all.

I guess I'm letting go of fear of being hurt; fear of poverty; fear of abandonment. I accept safety, love and prosperity. I am safe, I am loved, I am prosperous.

5-22-06

At therapy today I fell into a vortex, a space within my feelings and found my deep shame or vileness and it held nothing, this place in me is an illusion the therapist said, and I can see that, the shame and guilt and pain I carry is Dad's. I even carry shame for B—she held out both arms demonstrating holding something in both hands doesn't allow me to reach out for my own life. I was amazed by the psychic work, going into the shame and having nothing there. It was hot. Buzzy. Constricted. And there was nothing there. The therapist said that it was because it was an illusion. The illusion is I'm the vile one when really it is my stepfather, and why does he get invited to the party? She asked why family members know and still invite him? I think it is because it is a secret still—or somehow my forgiveness makes it okay. Lets him have his honor still. I had power when I wasn't forgiving, or perhaps I'm still empowered by forgiving, but he has to stand outside now while I take my place inside. We did good work today—very good work. Once I got home I ate a big lunch. I was exhausted and I've been eating substantial amounts ever since. A friend of mind says she thinks that Mary Magdalene energy is alive with the movie coming out, Da Vinci Code—and the strangeness lately is part of it—or caused by the discussion around Jesus and Mary. I don't know about that, but I did have a psychic healing today. My guides must have helped, because something definitely happened; it was powerful.

5-23-2006

I was awakened early this morning by a rumbling cement truck. I have been lying here, now, falling in and out of sleep, for over an hour, feeling too tired to get up. The work I did yesterday with the therapist was intense. That valley inside where the vileness lived is empty now. This morning I saw the valley filling with light. And this morning, instead of seeing my mother closed off to me in my mind's eye, I saw her smiling and caring for me from beyond the veil. So now I have her back, too. I know now that I'm in a process that I can't hurry. I'm unraveling the last little bits of my hidden parts.

Now I have the challenge of divorcing before me. Maybe not this summer, maybe not until next year.

MORTON J. MILLER

Letters from the Dog

Dear Sis,

I suppose that you will be somewhat surprised to receive a letter from me since I've never written to you before, but as they say every dog has his day and today is my day for letter writing. I really would have written sooner but I've had that fungus infection on my paws and it made it hard for me to type. However, I'm okay now and I can hit the keys without any trouble.

I must say that I do miss you. I jumped around in your room for two weeks in the morning before I realized that you weren't there, and that I'd have to get Dad up to let me out. And that's a bit dangerous because every once in a while I wake Mom instead and you know how she is when you wake her before eleven o'clock. On Tuesday I was innocently barking at a passing garbage truck, and I woke her. Boy, did she blow her cool. She opened one pink eye, glared at me and said, "one more yip and I'll trade you in for a couple of goldfish." Man, did I get under that bed in a hurry.

I still haven't quite gotten over spending last weekend at the Vet's. Sleeping Beauty and the Prince went to New York for the weekend, so old Bailie got farmed out to the Langman Hilton. I understand you're complaining about Ellen…you should have seen what was in charge of my cage. Our counsellor was some flea-bitten mutt who looked like Sandy from Orphan Annie. You know, he had those big blank eyes, that stupid look, and he kept bouncing around yelling Arf Arf. What a fink.

Well, I've got to go now. Fiddle and I are going to trot over to the Schultze's house and knock over a few garbage cans. You can never tell, there might be a good roast beef bone in there somewhere. And then we're going across the street and pee on those yapping chihuahuas. Maybe old Tinker will join us if the fuzz doesn't get him. Love from Mom, Dad, and Andy.

Love,

Bailie

August 7, 1969

Nan Baby,

Thought you might be ready for a few scribbles from El Poocho. Was going to write sooner, but the damn ticks have been driving me out of my skull. And if they aren't bad enough, I've also got to put up with our dear Father who is always going over me trying to find them. To use a lousy pun, he really bugs me, or should I say de-bugs me. And all that scratching around tickles. Maybe that's where the word tickle comes from—from feeling someone for ticks, yuk, yuk! And speaking of ticks, did you know they found some on the moon? They're called luna-ticks. Yuk, Yuk, Yuk! But enough of these rotten jokes. I want to tell you what happened yesterday.

It's about nine o'clock in the AM and I'm coming back from my morning walk when a police car pulls up and two fuzz get out. Well, you know how it is Nan, I've been busted before, and I figure if I'm a two-time loser it's into the pound and they throw away the key. If I wasn't already white I would have turned white. I was scared. The one cop starts to grab me, and I sort of dodge, but you know Old Bailie isn't exactly Jack-be-Nimble. He does get me and they throw me into the Patrol Car. It's all over, Bailie, Baby. I think, there's no way out now. But just at that moment there's a tremendous crash and the police car gets knocked off the street and into a tree. It's pretty badly wrecked, and the fuzz is kind of banged up, but they manage to stumble out of it and they stagger toward the blue Buick that ran into them. I'll bet I don't have to give you more than one guess as to who was driving that Buick. You're right, it was good old Grandpa Harry, the worst driver this side of the Atlantic. Well, Nan, that saves this little Scotch doggie's hide. I'm sort of woozy myself, but while the cops are arguing with Grandpa Harry, I get the heck out of there and, if you'll pardon the pun, high tail it home.

I haven't found out yet what finally happened with Gramps and the fuzz because I've been afraid to go out of the house, but I'll let you know in my next letter.

Love,

Bailie

Wednesday

Nan Baby,

I guess it's about time for you to get a little scribbling from the Westie-who's—the-Bestie, namely yours truly. I would have put paw to paper before this, but I've been bugged clean out of my skull by all the thunder storms we've been having.

Like last night. I'm home all alone when one of those storms starts. Big Morgan and Jolly Judy are at the movies, Andy is at a friends, and good old lonesome Bailie is minding the homestead as usual. Since no one is home I'm catching a fast forty on the sofa when all of a sudden there is a thunder clap that rattles dishes clear over to Macungie, and all the lights go out. Well, I almost went out of my skin. I leap off the sofa like I'm trying to set the Olympic broad-jump record, and since it's dark, I crack my head on the coffee table. That stuns me a bit, but then there is another lightning flash and a tremendous blast of thunder, and I snap out of it real quick. By now my chin is trembling, my eyes are rolling, and before I know it I've peed a puddle in the middle of the living room carpet. Now I figure it's really endsville, because if the storm doesn't kill me Mom will, and I'm only wondering which would be a better way to go. But it wasn't endsville. Just then the door opens and in walk the Grandparents, Ethel and Harry. Since it's so dark and I'm so upset I think it's burglars, and I take a fast bite out of the nearest leg, which turns out to be Ethel's. Zap!!! She lets out a shriek that makes the thunder sound like a cap pistol. "Harry" she screams, "that rotten dog bit me." "Not only doesn't he say hello, but he bit me." "Chang would never do that." "Even little Chiffon wouldn't do that to me."

Well, Nan Baby, I guess you can see the spot I'm in; if I stay in the house I'm liable to get killed by the Grandparents, and if I go outside, it's stormsville U.S.A. I know I've got to split, but where, and how? You've got to admit it's a mind-bending situation. But luck was with old Bailie that night. At that moment Uncle Norman and Taffy drive up to visit. They come into the house and just as the lights come on Taffy bites Ethel on the other leg. Pow!!! Grandma lets out another shriek. Grandpa smacks Taffy on the head with a chicken he is carrying, and I'm saved because they all think Taffy bit Ethel the first time too. And when the folks come home a few minutes later there is so much excitement that they don't even notice that I've peed on the carpet.

So, Nan Baby that's why I haven't written before this. I hope you're having a good summer. See you soon.

Love,

Bailie

Nancy Darling,

I'm sorry that I haven't written to you sooner sweetheart, but you know how bad my eyes are, and how hard it is for me to see what I am writing. So I am having this letter typed by one of the little girls in your daddy's office, a girl named Carrie Helen, or Marie Ellen or something like that.

The main reason I am writing sweetheart, is that I saw a copy of the letter that that rotten dog wrote to you – why your parents keep an awful animal like that around the house I will personally never understand. He's got a funny tail, his hair is always covering his eyes so he doesn't even know where he's going, and he has a disposition that makes Nasser seem like an angel. And always he is going around in circles. Who needs such a mutt? Believe me I'm not sensitive but when a full grown dog can't even say hello to his own grandmother, it's pretty awful. You know how Chiffon loves me, and as for Chang he adores me. Just yesterday he sat there in your Aunt's house and licked the very ground where my feet were. And believe me, it had nothing to do with the fact that I spilled a bowl of chicken soup on the floor. He just loves me.

But anyway Sweetheart, I saw the letter that that miserable mutt wrote to you, and I want you should know my side of the story. In the first place, I know very well that he was the one who bit me and not that poor Taffela, who wouldn't even bother a fly. In the second place I did not shriek. Refined ladies don't shriek, and I certainly never do. In the third place, I didn't call Chiffon an idiot, or at least she is smart enough not to bite her own grandmother, which is more than you can say for some other rotten animal whose name I wouldn't mention. And in the fourth place, it was not a chicken that Grandpa Harry hit Taffy with. You know very well that your Grandfather does not walk around carrying chickens. It was really a smoked herring, and it's a shame that he had to waste it to hit a dog with.

So darling, I just wanted you should know that that dog of yours tells lies and you shouldn't believe a word he says. And I assure you it will be a long time before I sing "Won't You Come Home Bill Bailey" to him again. Any dog who thinks his own Grandmother is a burglar and bites her doesn't deserve you should sing songs to him.

I hope you are having a good time, sweetheart. Give my love to all the kids in the bink or the bunk or whatever it is.

Love,

Dear Nan Baby,

Just thought you might like a few lines from your favorite Westie. There really isn't much to write, because with you away the house has been dullsville. The only thing jumping around here are the fleas on yours truly, and even they are taking it easy for the summer.

But we do get a little action. Like yesterday those Jones kids and their parents came over. You know Dick the Menace and his sister Alice the Animal. Man, are they a drag! Anyway, it's a quiet Sunday afternoon. The lord and master is out golfing, Mom is reading, and I'm out in the yard trying to get some sun on my nose when they arrive. The first thing I know, this Alice creep pours a bucket of cold water on me and yells, "wake up doggie." Well, I woke up all right, and I'm about to sink the old canines in her leg when her brother raps me on the nose with a wiffle bat. Man, did I see stars. I let out a yowl that they hear all over the neighborhood, and with that their old lady comes out. "Is that nasty dog bothering you?" she says, and Dickie says "yeah, this mean old wolf wants to bite little red riding hood," and he gives me another rap on the nose. By now I figure I'm a gone dog, but at that moment Grandma Ethel comes around the corner. She takes one look at me, claps her hands and starts singing 'Won't You Come Home Bill Bailey'. God, how I hate all the jerks who sing that to me. Anyway, this sort of stops the kids, and I figure maybe I'm saved, but then Alice yells "save me Dickie, it's the wicked witch of the West", and Dickie belts Grandma Ethel on the nose with the wiffle bat. Pandemonium! The wicked witch of the West gives out with a "Vey is Mir" that rattles windows three blocks away, and I turn even whiter than I am. I stick my tail between my legs and take off like the dog-fuzz is after me, and I don't stop until I'm across Tilghman Street. By the time I come home three hours later the Jones are gone, Ethel has an ice bag on her nose, and when she spots me she says "see, Bill Bailie did come home." What a blast!!!

Well Nan baby, that's about the long and the short. I can't wait for you to make the scene here; it's been a long summer. Love from your sore-nosed dog.

Bailie

FROM THE DESK OF BAILIE MILLER

Tuesday

Dear Nancy,

You should have seen what they did to me yesterday! Just because I was scratching my belly Mom took me to that quack, Fuhrman. He decided that I had an allergy. Imagine! First he gave me some kind of crazy bath to make me stop itching, then he gave me a shot. He also gave me some pills to take for three weeks. Dad gave me one of them hidden in a small piece of salami tonight, and he thought I didn't notice it, but I did.

The Lebovitz's came home today, a day late because their plane had to go to Boston because it couldn't land in New York. Peter and Jimmy came over and they said they had a great time.

Monday's and Tuesday's comics are enclosed. Please save them because Andy wants to put them all up on his bulletin board.

I hope you're having fun.

Love,

Bailie

Friday

Dear Nancy,

Last night I changed the filter in your fish tank, and one of the guppies bit me. It was the small one with the beady, bloodshot eyes. It wasn't a bad bite, but he did take off about half of my nail, and a tiny bit of my finger. It was on my left hand though, so it's nothing to worry about. Also, Bailie has found out that one of the fish is a cat fish, and now he keeps chasing it around the tank. It's really a funny sight to see that big dog running around inside of that little tank. And he splashes water all over the room. I just hope that one of the guppies doesn't bite him.

Have you received the boots, Cutes? Answer!!!

Love from Mom, Mongrel, and Me.

Dad

June 26, 1967

Dear Miss Miller:

This is to inform you that you are being put on our mailing list to receive a two month subscription to Krazy Kamp Letters. These letters and cards will contain our usual assortment of utter nonsense, useless information, and terrible jokes. Since the publisher of Krazy Kamp Letters happens to be your father, you will be expected to read every one. Some of the letters will contain requests for information that you will have to supply by return mail. Of course, you will be tested when you return from camp to see how much you remember. And it had better be plenty.

We trust that you will have a most wonderful summer, and that you will enjoy this year's edition of Krazy Kamp Letters.

Affectionately yours,

Morton J. Letterwriter

P.S. There will be a slight charge of twenty seven kisses for this service, to be paid by you during visiting weekend at camp. Thank you.

Monday

Miss Nancy Miller
Camp Mataponi
Naples Maine

Dear Miss Miller,
We are presently conducting a survey to determine how many people would be interested in our new book Training Wasps for Fun & Profit. If you believe that you would be interested, please return the enclosed card and you will receive the book and a free supply of wasps.

Since our supply of wasps is limited, we suggest that you act immediately. In the event that wasps are not available, we will provide hornets instead. Thank you.

Very truly yours,

Morton J Wasptrainer

Thursday

Dear Madam,

The book you have taken from the library, Shearing Sheep with a Cuticle Scissors, is now three weeks overdue. Unless you return this book at once, you will be subject to a fine of seven cents per day. In addition, your special privileges will be cancelled, and you will not be allowed to pop bubble gum in the library reading room. This book is one of our more popular ones, and thousands of sheep are going unclipped because people do not have the book that you are selfishly keeping. Please return it at once. Thank you.

> Stroudsburg Public Library
> Stroudsburg, Pa.
> Morton J. Bookwork III

We are Filling your Order

Madame:
XXXXXX   Date August 15, 1967

In reply to your inquiry dated July 19, 1967

Please be advised that we expect to make shipment of goods on your

Order No. 25759   Dated   July 16, 1967

On or about August 26, 1967

Remarks: As soon as mice are born we will ship them.
> Yours very truly,
> Mixedup Mouse Co.
> Portland, Maine.

STANDARD FORM 100

Howard Johnson's
Host of the Highways

POST CARD
MISS NANCY MILLER
CAMP MATAPONI
NAPLES, MAINE

DEAR MISS MILLER,
CONGRATULATIONS, YOU
HAVE BEEN VOTED QUEEN
OF THE CLAM FESTIVAL.
YOU WILL BE PICKED UP IN
A COACH DRAWN
BY SIX LOBSTERS. AT MIDNIGHT
THEY TURN INTO A DISH OF
LOBSTER NEWBURG. HAPPY
EATING! MORTON J. JOHNSON

Dear Niece Nancy,

I hope you remember me. I am your great Uncle Edgar who resides in Florida. The last time I saw you. You were three years old and you were sitting in the kitchen sink blowing bubbles. I have often wondered why any little girl would sit in a sink blowing bubbles. The next time I see you I will ask why. I hope you are enjoying camp. Love, Uncle Edgar

MORTON J. MILLER

Monday

Dear Nan,

Well, we are back from our weekend in New York. Mom and I went in on Saturday to attend the Green wedding and we got home late last night. We stayed at the Cohens, who send you their love. The weather wasn't great, but we did get a chance to do a little swimming in their pool. The wedding itself was nice, and we had a good time. On the way home yesterday we stopped in Elizabeth to see Grandma Hilda. Grandpa Bill has gone to Europe and so she is home alone and a bit lonesome. She may come out to Allentown for a few days next week.

Tonight the Monkeys are giving a concert in Allentown. As a matter of fact, they are going to perform in the trees across the street from the house. There will fourteen of them in the group, some playing instruments, some singing, and some just swinging by their tails from the branches. On three of the numbers they will be joined by the Limits. That's Sam and Morris Limits, who just look like Monkeys and play the Harpsichord and Spanish guitar. They are going to play all their good songs like Shleppin' Stones (Is Hard Work), The Day We Fall in the Cesspool, Hairy, Hairy, and their latest hit Your Auntie Gorilla. It's too bad you have to miss it cause it sounds like it's gonna be real wild.

I am enclosing todays adventure of Nancy, which I am sure you will enjoy.

Are you or are you not taking riding lessons? You keep asking about the hat, but you haven't told us whether you are riding. Please, a little information in your next letter.

Since there are two of you Nancy Susan Millers in the camp, I would suggest that you let us know what bunk you are in so that we can address our letters that way. Also, if you know it include the Zip Code number.

I sent you some hair pins today which you should receive in a few days.

Love, love, love, love, love, love, love,

Dad

MILLCREST MANUFACTURING CO.
Manufacturers of Sleepwear and Allied Products

946 Seneca Street Bethlehem, Pa. 18015 Telephone (215) 865-5391

Tuesday

Dear Nan,

I gather from the card you wrote on Saturday that the Fuzz

appropriated the contents of the package I sent to you. Too Bad!!! It was a real goodie. Inside that little box were 2497 calories of the greatest Viennese Sausage that a camper ever laid tooth to. There were great big beautiful chunks of it swimming in a safflower and bacon-rind sauce that you had to smell to believe. Just thinking of it I have to cover my mouth to keep from drooling all over the typewriter. I just can't understand how the heartless bastards could keep it from you. But don't worry! Your Dad is a fighter and doesn't quit so easily. I have sent to New York for another batch of the stuff and I'm going to smuggle it into you disguised as a bunch of creepy crawlers. Enjoy!

The weather being what it is (it seldom is what it isn't), I guess you are getting rain checks instead of bed checks. What are you kiddies doing while Jupe is Pluving? One of the best ways to kill time on rainy days is to put on little plays. A favorite of many girl campers is Joan of Arc. Most of it is dullsville, but the part where you tie a counselor to the stake and set her on fire is usually good for a few yuks. It's even more fun if you toast marshmallows on her while singing I Don't Want to Set the World On Fire. This little gem and many other goodies are all in a little book called Rainy Day Games For Camp and the Funny Farm. Send me a lock of your hair and I'll mail you a copy.

Keep your powder dry and don't eat any wooden pickles.

Much L*O*V*E
Pappy Hokum

MORTON J. MILLER

Tuesday

Dear Love of My Life,

Today's letter will consist of a list of all the words you have spelled wrong in your cards and letters, and God knows there have been enough of them. If you are not the world's worst speller, you are pretty close to it. You're just lucky that you make up for it by being so pretty. In any case, here is the list, with your spellings and the correct ones:

Nancy's Spellings	Correct Spellings
Horse	Hoarse
Aloud	Allowed
Shampo	Shampoo
Seramices	Ceramics
Tenis	Tennis
Mett	Met
Saterday	Saturday
Tobeehana	Tobyhanna

Love from Mom.
Much love,

Dad

Wednesday

Dear Nan,

I was going to write you one of those silly letters about the strange animals who came to live with us, but I decided that this year you are too old to believe that sort of nonsense. Besides, I just don't have the time. I've been very busy since you left trying to teach a silk worm to become a nylon worm. Unfortunately, this particular worm is not too bright, and he just can't get the hang of making nylon. Sometimes he makes rayon, and every once in a while he makes a little dacron, but most of the time he just makes silk. The worms name, by the way, is Michael, which is causing all kinds of mix-ups, because every time I talk to the worm, Michael Schwab thinks that I am talking to him. Yesterday morning things got so mixed up that the worm went to day camp, and Michael Schwab stayed home and made silk. Aunt Ruth thought it was a good idea, and she is now trying to get him to spin himself a giant cocoon and hibernate until it is time to go back to school. By the way, if you are wondering why I'm doing all this it's very simple. If it works, I'm going to get sixty thousand more silk worms and teach them all to be nylon worms, and they will make all

the cloth for our nightgown factory. Of course it will be quite a job to feed and care for sixty thousand nylon worms, but I think you might be just perfect for the job. If you think you'd like to do it write to me, and I'll send you a book on the care and feeding of nylon worms. Incidentally, the job will pay 29 cents a week
     Love from your mother and canine brother.

Xxxxxxxxxxxxxxxxx
Love,

Dad

                    Morton J. Miller
                    3030 Tremont St.
                    Allentown,Penna

April 10, 1958
The President of the United States
The White House
Washington, D.C.

Mr. President:
In reference to your remarks at your Press Conference of Wednesday, April 9, 1958, I would like to point out my wife, Mrs. Morton Miller, as a patriotic citizen who is doing her utmost to help curb the current recession. So strenuous have been her efforts to alleviate this unfortunate situation, that I feel she is due special recognition. In a time when most people are retrenching, she has selflessly increased her rate of spending so that it currently approximates that of the government itself.
     While it is quite obvious that spending such as my wife's has a direct salutary effect on our economy, I would also like to point out a very important side effect. Due entirely to my wife's frenetic efforts,

I, a manufacturer of ladies sleepwear, have been forced to substantially increase my sales and production in a desperate effort to keep pace with her. The result has been that I have given more people employment, put more money into circulation and generally helped to promote economic recovery.

In light of the foregoing, I think it would be entirely appropriate for the government to show its appreciation to Mrs. Miller. Not that she seeks rewards or personal aggrandizement as she quietly goes about her chosen task. But perhaps, a "Pat on the Back", a "Well Done" or simple "Thank You" will let her know that her efforts have not been unappreciated and may spur other women to like achievements.

Incidentally, Mrs. Miller is a registered Republican.

Very respectfully yours,
Morton J. Miller

MJM/bjm

Nancy Dear,

Once, when I was twelve years old, I was tending the goats in my father's oat field. After the goats had eaten half of the oats my father appeared and said; "Fool, why have you let the goats eat the oats?" "I'm sorry, Father," I said, but the goats were hungry, and soon they will go to sleep, and I did not want them to sleep on an empty stomach." My father looked at me silently for a moment, and then he spoke very slowly. "Jacob", he said, using my middle name, which he did when he was angry or sad, "Jacob, if all the goats on earth went to sleep hungry tonight, would the world spin any faster tomorrow?"

Gail Reitano

Growing up (Italian) in the New Jersey Pine Barrens

"We had five whole acres, a good part of which was second-growth bush, studded with blueberries, which the little Italian children who were our neighbors picked and sold back to us."
-- from Margaret Mead's memoir "Blackberry Winter"

Mead came to our town of Hammonton, New Jersey, brought there as a child by her mother, Emily Fogg Meade, who was conducting a study of the Italian immigrant.

Our neighbors, the Seeleys, were friends of Margaret Mead's and the famous anthropologist sometimes visited. One cold February morning Mom streamed into the kitchen. "Margaret Mead is out on the paddleboat with Mrs. Seeley!" she announced with excitement. She tried to get me to walk with her down to the lake, but it was cold and overcast and I was home from college and making myself breakfast. I was also feeling my power and wanting to deny my mother, who hadn't gone to college, the satisfaction of demonstrating her knowledge. Because of course she knew exactly what Margaret Mead looked like, just as she would have recognized John Kenneth Galbraith or George Plimpton, just as she once saw Lillian Hellman in the sculpture garden of the Museum of Modern Art in New York and had almost spoken to her. "I wanted to say how much I loved Pentimento but she was eating her lunch."

A week later the local paper wrote about how Mrs. Seeley had taken her friend Margaret Mead out on her paddleboat on the Hammonton Lake. My mother clipped the article and sent it to me.

**

I was called on to read from our 4th grade American History book, a section about immigrants. I cleared my throat and began, not fully understanding the words, and of course I had failed to read it the night before, though that had been the assignment. When I came to the phrase "an undigested and indigestible element in our body politic, and a constant menace to our free institutions" I was jolted from my fog. Not that I fully understood the words, not that I thought our history book could possibly include anything pertaining to me, but that I caught a familiar whiff of that something Mom sometimes complained about.

That year we studied the Pompeian ruins and those beautiful bodies found in poses resembling sleep. Fulminant shock, I learned, was when a body was struck dead as it lived, before there was time for conscious reaction. Mom said that as a teenager my great grandmother would look up at Mount Vesuvius and wonder whether she would be in Italy long enough to see it explode again. As it happened she wouldn't; she would make her way to this country, escaping poverty and volcanoes, and the way she would avoid a different set of hazards once she got here was by not learning English and remaining indoors.

**

Whenever my father felt the need to impress someone, including his three daughters, out came the story of how his father, Jimmy Reitano, once owned the famous Bookbinder's Restaurant in Philadelphia, and with each telling the story was further embellished with the names of movie stars, famous ball players and the club owners to whom Jimmy served steak and seafood dinners.

How he acquired the restaurant was like this. In 1946, Jimmy had Bookbinder's appraised before approaching a man named Hyman Cycle. It was a time when few people had much money, but Mr. Cycle had made his fortune through lucrative war contracts. According to Dad, Mr. Cycle provided every mattress that went on board every navy ship at Sun Shipyard in Chester, Pennsylvania, and Mr. Cycle liked my grandfather and so agreed to back him.

Jimmy rose early to go down to the docks, where he hand-picked sirloins, fillets, ribs and chops. He did all the meat buying, and he had a natural talent for spotting the right degree of marbling, the most tender cuts. His unerring judgment attracted a first class clientele, and put Bookbinder's, what had long been a losing operation, into the black in the first year.

Jimmy's first job had been counting ice cars arriving by rail into Philadelphia's 30th Street Station. But when he became the co-owner of a famous restaurant he began driving a Peerless.

Dad would never take us to Bookbinder's. If there was some painful history surrounding how Jimmy "lost" the restaurant, to this day I don't know. I remember once Mom suggested we all go. "Why not take the girls," she said. "Nooo, Lorraine." He shook his head, which was her signal to drop the subject.

**

I was very young, on a beautiful spring day in 1961 when Mom and I stood next to Uncle, and the three of us looked up at the façade of the old Rivoli Theatre.

Samuel Frank built the Rivoli Theatre on Hammonton's main street in 1927. With a façade that was designed to imitate the Ducal Palace in Venice, and named after the famous Rivoli Theater in New York on 49th and Broadway, the theatre boasted 450 seats, including 250 balcony seats.

According to the Manager's Report, March 28, 1941:

Type of Patronage: Small town, farmers and mill workers. Poor class of Italians.

Balcony for Colored?: Yes.

"I'm buying it, Lorraine," Uncle said.

I tugged at the soft fabric of his jacket. "What about the movie theater, Uncle Lewis?"

"What about it, darling?"

"Are you going to open it again so we can go see movies?"

Mom's painful squeeze of my hand told me I wasn't to persist.

Uncle did buy the Rivoli, but he didn't reopen the theater. Instead he pierced his fortress with large planes of glass, installed gold trimmed doors and clad the entire building in Carrara marble.

Television was given credit for killing the neighborhood theater, but the automobile did just as much to end the local cinema, so it was perhaps fitting that Uncle replaced the old Rivoli with his automobile finance company. It made him a fortune, because from the time the boys first returned home from the war they needed to finance everything, starting with their cars.

**

Everyone at school knew I lived at The Harbour and that my aunt and uncle had money. So it was easy for me to refine an air of importance, especially as my sisters and I liked to roam the place like so many fugitive princesses.

"Watch for me around twelve-thirty, darlings," Uncle said.

My two sisters and I were in the pool—in Aunt and Uncle's pool down the lane from our more modest house—and we were getting ready to wave.

My arms were half out of the water as I heard the plane droning in the distance. Uncle's small Cessna made a wide loop and buzzed us twice, flying frighteningly low over the tallest pines. I tried to pick him out behind the glass of the cockpit, but he was gone in a second. The plane's departure left a hole of sound I filled with energetic strokes as I pulled through the water with greater purpose.

**

The house my parents built was a long, low ranch like a train come to rest. It was generous and well-built but it always struck me as too plain. The Irish yew my father planted along the front were either dwarfs or refused to grow, and even once the trees had grown up, our house retained its bare appearance.

Mom employed a cleaning girl who scrupulously swept and dusted her carefully chosen sculptures and knick-knacks, the result of many influences from the style and living magazines of the time and a large, glossy coffee table book she especially loved, My Favorite Things by Dorothy Rodgers, wife of the songwriter. The book was full of large, bright Connecticut rooms full of color and valuable art.

Mom filled the long wall of our den with picks from the Book of the Month Club. She took art lessons from a nun who taught her how to paint with a knife and spread the oils on impasto. In this style she captured Kennedy looking pensive and handsome, his right hand resting on the middle button of his jacket. In another my sisters and I are doe-eyed and startled where we sit side by side at the piano. She often said, had her parents had enough money to send her to college she would have studied history. She liked stories of peasants in Europe, and people who had descended from all manner of strife and hardship. But she especially loved tales of the privileged, monarchies and royalty, and anything about the Duke and Duchess of Windsor.

Mom liked to say she was Carol Kennicott, the young wife with dreams of escape from Sinclair Lewis's Main Street, which meant Hammonton, New Jersey must have seemed to her like Gopher Prairie.

**

We were all girls in the packing house. Pop-pop's farm didn't have a conveyor belt, so everything that had to be lifted—like the heavy flats of blueberries—was lifted by us. But we were young and strong, and we ate a lot of berries while we packed.

I loved the hard physical work, and I loved being with people so removed from the social pecking order of Hammonton, with the never ending question, which Italians were better than the so-and-so's. And weren't we better than most?

A full pint packed and ready was dropped into the splintery crate. The hairy wood was scratchy and hard on our hands, snagging our knuckles, and at the end of the day our fingertips were black with dirt, the nails stained a deep blue around their edges. Another girl and I competed to see who could pack the fastest, an undeclared contest, fierce and determined, but occasionally one of us would grab a quick glance at the other and we'd burst out laughing.

The year is 1964 and there is a picture of my grandfather holding up a branch from one of his blueberry bushes. Behind him is a vast clear sky; underneath that is his farm. You can't believe how large the berries are!

In 1916, a man named Frederick Coville successfully bred the highbush cultivars my grandfather would plant on his farm forty years later: Blueray, Bluecrop, Coville, Jersey, Berkeley and Weymouth—which Pop-pop considered his money crop—all of which are still grown today.

Sometimes we'd steal out to the tomato patch to pick the ripest of the ripe to eat on the spot. We'd take a saltshaker kept on top of the refrigerator out to the field so we could salt up before every bite.

**

It was a warm night with fire flies lighting like stars. Dad came outside and asked me if I wanted to gig some frogs. I said I did even though I didn't know what gigging was.

Ransom's pond was a huge oval still as glass and a worn path ran along the waterline. Without a word Dad handed me the "gig," a three-pronged spear attached to a broom handle. He whispered that I was to hold it just so. Next he dragged the flashlight's beam along the pond's white bottom where we caught sight of a frog. I crept forward on the balls of my feet and aimed for the dead center of its back.

"Now!" he ordered.

I plunged the stick down, but my second's hesitation was enough to allow the frog to spring away in a blur of water.

"You missed it!" He was disappointed I could tell.

We trudged around the pond a second time, but I knew Dad would take over and I wouldn't get another chance. "We'll get a couple more and go home." He managed to get four more big ones.

According to Dad the frogs had to be skinned alive. But after watching him skin the first two, I had to go into the house. I couldn't watch that hasty slice across the frog's middle, then clear around its back like halving a peach, and how Dad's strong hands with the sprouting black hairs, pulled the skin down in one great coat. The frogs twitched the whole time, until their lower halves hung denuded and gray.

"Look at that!" he exclaimed, tossing the legs into a swirling pan of butter and garlic. Minutes later we sat across from each other at the kitchen table scoffing them down.

**

It was the era of Julia Child.

"Guess what a boy on the bus said?"

"What?" Mom looked up from the French Chef Cookbook, her blond-streaked hair rigid with an elegant indignation that was something of a signature. She smiled. I could tell she hadn't even heard.

"This boy said Uncle Lewis is going to jail."

"Who said that?" She looked up.

I named him, then waited for her to give the usual balm of comfort, to say that the boy was the sorry product of the ignorant so-and-so's. I waited as her fingers rubbed the page of the recipe she'd been reading as if the smoothness of the paper was of some comfort.

"Well I guess everyone knows."

"Knows what?"

"About your uncle's troubles."

"What troubles?"

She stared at me. "Something with stocks. There might be a trial."

"Like in a courtroom?"

She crinkled her chin and gave me a Pop-pop look. She and her father had the same chin, and they were masters at a certain undisguised look of regret.

**

Stiletto, from stilo, Italian for dagger.

Margaret Mead's mother wrote how there were newspaper stories about us—Italians—in which "the stiletto is in evidence."

Thank god for the British who took the word and recast it as a high heel, which was how I first came to think about this word. I loved the shoes, and wore them without regard to how their blade-like shape might have resonated dangerously with my ancestors. The weapon of choice among my people was also the weapon of choice among women who couldn't get power any other way.

**

Whenever I went places with Pop-pop, we traveled by flatbed truck or pick-up. One day when he took me to visit the junkyard—that's exactly what he said, "Let's go visit the junkyard," he introduced me to Bozarth, descended from French Huguenots and who called himself a Piney. Yet he looked just like my grandfather, the same in their soiled work clothes and straw hats, of similar height and build—both were about six feet tall—and both had thick rinds of black dirt underneath their fingernails.

Bozarth's tiny cabin was made of the same scrap corrugated metal as Pop-pop's farm buildings, and belched a similar smoke from an identical pot belly stove.

There wasn't any sense to be made of who or what we were, when a man like Bozarth, who was after all French, and who I later found out came from a wealthy family, would choose to live down the end of a narrow dirt road and rarely speak more than a few words.

When we got home, Mom announced that one of her literary puzzles was selected to be published in The Saturday Review. It made me wonder how it all squared, and the answer was, it didn't. Until slowly, with a child's eye, I began to understand the impulse to travel past all cultures in search of that one beautiful field.

**

After the Depression, Pop-pop had worked as a truck driver running sugar up to the illegal stills, back and forth between Philadelphia and Boston, and that was how he saved up enough money to buy the farm. It was no secret either that Grammy took a job at Waldman's pants factory to make extra money. One day, as Grammy twirled a pants leg around to work on its inseam, the building collapsed on top of her, and a broken pipe filled a trough of water where she and four other women lay for hours. Grammy's neck was permanently damaged.

The day she told me the story, I was seven or eight years old, I felt like I'd discovered I was from a completely different family from the one I thought. Afterward, I followed her around her flower garden on the farm. She was dressed in her favorite clothes, jodhpurs, neckerchief and crisp white blouse. She looked just like her favorite actress, Barbara Stanwyck, in Cattle Queen of Montana.

**

The empty swimming pool was visible from the small dormer of our apartment, what had been the former servants quarters over the garage, and each morning I stared longingly past the flagstone path to the cracked and faded rectangle of blue.

Finally, because it was summer, and we were anxious to swim, Dad gave the go ahead for the inebriated gardener to fill the pool. I, at least, was serenaded by the clatter of water that continued for three days and nights, and woke on that final day to the same excitement I'd felt as a child. When I took my first look at the full pool, the water was crystalline just as I remembered. Then, for two whole days, my husband, our small daughter and I did nothing but swim. On the third day, I woke and rushed to look out. But instead of dazzling aquamarine, there was the pool that in the night had formed on its surface what looked like a skin on old food.

Dad, my husband and I stood on the cold, cement floor of the pump house smelling of gasoline, and together we eyed the broken pump. I wanted to suggest a new filter, but braced instead for Dad's long drawn out cheap solution, which we would try first. A new filter would not only cost money, it would require a call down to his sister, Aunt Maddy, in Florida, who despite the fortune Uncle had left her, never liked to spend a cent.

I imagined their conversation.

Dad: "Maddy, the girls want to swim."

Maddy: "Who cares about that old mausoleum."

**

I was fifteen when I made my first swim across the Hammonton lake, a near quarter mile I braved by pacing my strokes, parting the cedar-colored water alive in my hands. I wasn't supposed to swim in the lake or in Aunt and Uncle's pool without letting someone know. For lake excursions I usually took my row boat, but that day even if it meant the risk of snapping turtles—snapper soup was on all the menus—I knew I would swim.

I reached the shore and was surprised to land on a tiny bank made of sugar sand, thought to have originated from sand dunes a million years old. It was this plain sugar that gave the barrens its name, as it supported only scrub, and farmers knew to avoid it.

Uncle owned the land underneath the lake and the bird preserve right behind me. I imagined a vast wilderness at my back, but what was really there beyond a narrow fringe of trees was the Egg Harbor Road, a two-lane speedway that ran past a defunct cookie factory called Deer Park and eventually connected to the White Horse Pike, a rural stretch of four-lanes dotted with old garages, farm stands and tattered billboards.

I had heard Uncle say he wanted to build on the preserve, which would involve breaking the former owners' will. From this other shore I gazed back at our dock and caught a glimpse of the mansion past a sweep of perfect lawn and the hot pink rhododendrons in full summer flower. The sight filled me with desire, and with a quiet splash, I slipped off the shore into the gentle moving water, and swam.

**

Growing up in the Pine Barrens I've seen and handled my share of pine cones. Played with them, had my fingers pricked by the pointy end of the cone scale, learned that fire opens their bracts and releases their seeds—so pines need fire. I learned something else about them the other day, something unusual that I came upon by accident.

This, from an article by Brother Alfred Brousseau, "Fibonacci Statistics in Conifers":

"The Editor of the *Fibonacci Quarterly* has received an urgent phone call from a Houghton-Mifflin representative: 'Is the picture of the pine cone in your manuscript spiraling correctly?' With such questions in mind, an investigation was begun in the summer of 1969. Very quickly it was discovered that spirals on cones go in both directions."

SHERRY STRATTON

Looking out the Window...Notes from a Year of Watching

February 13
Around 6:45 this morning, Dick heard me getting up and came in to tell me there were deer in the yard. I stood at the window with him as five deer gathered around Meadowbrook. All were smallish. Too early for spring flowers, so our pleasure was not mixed with the dismay of seeing our tulips munched to the ground.

April 4
For the past couple years, we've had a pair of mallards visiting Meadowbrook in the spring. We've usually seen them in the mornings, but this year's first appearance was at dinnertime. It was Mrs. Mallard, and from the time she landed in the pond, she never settled in: quack, quack, quacking constantly. Never dove for food or did anything except look around and quack. It was pretty clear she was quacking for Mr. M. What happened? Signals crossed? After a while, she flew off. Hope to see them both tomorrow and know that all is well.

April 5
Mr. Mallard was around for a while this morning, but no sign of the Mrs.

April 13
This morning as we were driving out to shop, I saw a skunk

foraging in a neighbor's yard. It was the yard with the immense manicured lawn, and the skunk was smack dab in the middle. Oblivious and quite lovely with its long bushy tail, healthy coat. (Woods kitty, as Dad would say.) I think of skunks as nocturnal and secretive. Only once before have I seen a wild skunk in the daytime. (In the forest preserve off a side trail—very busy with the severed foot of some creature.)

We have not seen our mallards, either one, since my last entry.

April 15

M. & M. Mallard were back in the yard this morning.

April 18

Ramona the raccoon came out early enough this evening for us to see her well. We're guessing, from how she looks, that she has given birth. She sat on the limb for some time doing the usual scratching and stretching. At one point I jumped up and went out to hiss away a stray cat from the yard, and when I came back in and checked Ramona again with binocs, she was clearly staring our way. We watched her climb down the tree by an unorthodox route and head out to hunt for the night.

May 1

Mid-afternoon we saw an injured coyote in the yard. We've seen this one before, holding up its right front limb. It ran across the back of the yard, stopping often and looking wary. Headed into the pines and disappeared from view. Around 4:00, saw M. & M. Mallard under the birdfeeder. Eventually they made their way into the pond.

May 4

Yesterday late afternoon I watched the mallard pair in Meadowbrook. She bobbed repeatedly, looking as though she was trying--and failing--to execute a surface dive. He stood guard. Today, about the same time, we saw them circle in and land next to the water. They proceeded into the pond and repeated the bobbing, bathing, preening routine.

May 14

Yesterday afternoon things started to really pop in the warbler department--at last. Here is what we were able to identify in a few minutes: palm, Cape May, Tennessee, yellow-rumped, common yellow throat. As I was swinging my binocs from warbler to warbler, a hummingbird appeared in startling close-up. This was the year's first hummer sighting, though the feeders have been in place for a week and a half. I'd been trying not to let the long stretch of cold spring get on my nerves. A day like this one helps.

May 26

Tonight, our first look at this year's Coonettes. Three of them came tumbling out onto the limb where Ramona was already stretched out (escaping, we think). She licked them and pawed them and soon enough nosed them back into the hollow. Not yet time for them to be about.

June 17

Correction: Ramona + four Coonettes

June 22

Make that five! Tonight Monie and her crew appeared on the limb, and the Coonettes lined up and held still so I could count them--five.

July 30

A tailless squirrel lives here in town. When I first spotted it, I was at a complete loss. All I could think was rabbit, but it didn't move like a rabbit. Nor did it move like a squirrel, exactly, and it certainly didn't look like one. (I could not have imagined how unlike a squirrel a squirrel looks without its tail.) I have seen it several more times, always within a block or so of that original spot, near the rec center. It catches me up every time. I puzzled over the oddness of its gait, and started watching other squirrels more closely. Normal squirrels, I noticed, don't much walk, except on a power line or tree limb. They move on the ground in hops, short or long. I have never seen this tailless one hop. Its movement is a labored-looking left side, right side affair. I watch for this squirrel now when I'm in its neighborhood, two or three times a week.

September 15

Sitting on the porch at dinnertime, we spotted a grosbeak on the birdfeeder. We see rose-breasted grosbeaks (RBG for short) mainly during migration. It's always a treat. This one was a female, or could it be a juvenile male? Something about its coloring was different; there was some yellow. An evening grosbeak? I focused on the notion of a new bird and looked more intently. Then with a sudden whoosh the grosbeak and a house finch flew from the feeder, and we heard a strike against the big kitchen window. Dick quickly declared that it was a glancing hit, but I was up and off to the kitchen. The bird was floating on its back in the birdbath, its body perfectly aligned. I saw pink under each wing. Dick went out and, picking it up by the tail, confirmed "it's the RBG." "It's dead?" I asked. "Yes." He walked across the yard, opened the shed with one hand and retrieved the shovel. He came back in and washed his hands, and we hugged. We finished dinner in silence, until Dick set down his fork and said, "I am so bothered by this." I said what I had been thinking, how swiftly our happy excitement had flipped to grief. And we talked about moving the feeder--yet again.

September 21

It is time to speak of my practice that I call "kicking out." I go around the yard, right before we mow, and kick at the grass with the sides of my shoes. The first time I did the mowing, I ran over a garter snake. That was what launched my kick-out practice, and I expect to continue it as long as we have grass to mow.

November 12

I was driving home on the main route through town, approaching the traffic light, when the tailless squirrel crossed the street right in front of me. So, it is still thriving, which I was happy to see. And I'm surprised as ever at the squirrel's strange appearance. Good that it happened to be me, a critter-conscious driver, I think. (Later, I think again. Not so good if I hadn't been able to stop.)

December

A buck with a big rack is standing in the yard, at high noon. He walks to the pond and bends down to drink. But then his hooves slide down the edge, and he stands awkwardly, looking stuck.

Eventually the deer drinks, then struggles back out of the water. He just stands there, and we realize something is wrong. When the deer finally starts walking, the going is slow, and we consider calling the forest preserve office. But a visitor is on her way over, and we need to finish lunch. The buck begins moving a bit faster; perhaps it's OK after all. A couple days later Dick talks to our neighbor, who's also been observing the buck. She says he has been sleeping near their house. She called the forest preserve, and two guys came out and tramped around, but left without finding him. It was a week or so later that I watched the dead buck being hauled by its antlers over the snow to the cul-de-sac and the waiting truck.

March 5

The tree trimming we had done on Tuesday has opened up the view from my study window. In winter, the river has always been visible from this west-facing window. But now, as the water flows at the edge of our neighbor's yard, I can see a wider swath. The dying pear tree, home to downy woodpeckers each spring, has been reduced to a stump. I'll miss it--well, not the tree so much, but the close-up, second-story view it gave me of those woodpeckers and other birds, too. I look out at the fresh, clean cuts on the locust tree, trimmed now to its crown. About 50 feet from the window and some 80 feet tall, this tree is now the nearest feature in my landscape. I wonder how much different my view will be once the trees are in leaf. What about the next tree west, in the neighbor's yard? I notice for the first time that the top of it looks dead, and now I am curious. Does any part of that tree ever become green? I am so accustomed to the river view being obscured in the green season that I haven't noticed exactly which greenery is in the way.

Yet another reason to look forward to spring.

FREDDI TACHMAN CARLIP

Footsteps

It's all Perspective

I live in an area where lawns are mowed every other day down to the brown nub. Bushes and shrubs are cut into organized shapes, standing like pruned sentries close to the overpriced boxes that pass for houses in developments with names like "Paris Meadows" and "The Summit" and "Countryside Estates." My 152-year-old farmhouse on 4 acres, including a pond is my sanctuary. I get asked, "Wow, you don't mind the overgrown back lawn? No, damn it, I don't! I love it. Keep your opinion to yourself. Go back to your manicured development. I'll revel in what I have here.

I see the beauty when others see the wildness. I look beyond the disrepair, the wildly growing trees and bushes. I see the pond, protected, beckoning to heron, ducks, geese, frogs, diving insects, muskrats, turtles. All are a joy to watch as they frolic. Feeling safe. The birds feeding by the house. Peeling paint. Wobbly roof. Rickety overhang. The birds don't mind nor do I. Food, water, a place to raise their young. I sit outside and I listen and observe. The covered pool with just enough water for the ducks to swim, for the foxes to drink. Soon the honeysuckle's fragrant flowers will burst forth and I will savor their essence.

Normal Mother

A few weeks ago, my ten-year-old daughter came home from school and stated emphatically that she was glad her friend's mother wasn't hers.

"You know what, Mom? She makes Alison clean the house after school. She couldn't play today because she had to clean." (I'm sure there was some hyperbole on my daughter's part.) "Besides, Mrs. S. wears rollers in her hair, plays golf, and watches soap operas. I'm glad I have a normal mother, like you."

Marcy's concept of "normal" refers to my running every day early in the morning, rain, sun, snow, every season of the year; going to the track for extra workouts; spending the day at a race, the highlight of which to Marcy is all the runners throwing up from the heat. "Normal" to Marcy means rows of running shoes and running clothes, the running of club meetings, and the running of the *Runner's Gazette* typesetter.

Footfalls on a Wednesday Evening

> Her shoes talk to her
>   As she runs
>   Each step brings the sound
>   Of a body in motion
>   Working muscles
>   Working mind
>
>   A second run
>   Quicker than the first
>   More focused
>   Bringing clarity
>   To her cluttered mind
> Peace to her jumbled emotions
>   Strength to her body
>
> She pays attention to the message
>   Each footfall brings-
>   Drink it in
>   Tuck away the sensations
>   The motion
>   The sweet sweat
>   Each breath

An experience for the senses
  Sensual
 Erotic
  Earthy

The essence of the senses-
  The feel of her body
  The smell of her sweat
  The taste of the air
  The visual feast
  The sounds from
   The sidewalk
The touch of life's velvet hand

Footfalls on a Wednesday evening
  Connecting her with life
    With living
   With the essence of
    Being alive
Footfalls on a Wednesday evening
  Bringing her closer to herself
Footfalls...

The Back Nine

In December, I was talking with a friend about my upcoming milestone birthday. Before I had a chance to tell her I'd be turning 60, she asked if I was turning 50. I told her that she was one decade early. She then made a comment that gave me a lot to think about. "You're on the back nine. Do what makes you happy."

I'm not a golfer, but I knew exactly what she meant: I'm on the back nine of life and I shouldn't squander the precious time in front of me. And, thanks to Laura, I'm doing my best to make my back-nine years the best years.

I've spent so many hours fretting over the future, or anticipating a significant occasion yet to come. I've lived with my planner, writing in dates and times as if my life was the planner. Some people call it "calendaring," living for the future, as we let each day escape our focus.

We might have thoughts like these: Once I get that marathon under my belt...once I get that 5K PR...once vacation comes...once the kids are out of school...once I get a new job...once I retire...then what?

The back nine—I'm aiming for a whole lot of holes-in-one.

In this game, we don't get a Mulligan after we play the last hole.

On the Verge of a 'Different Marathon'

The image of a woman I used to know is burned into my mind. She's the foundation upon which my life has been built. She helped me get to the starting line of the run that has become my life.

She entered college as an Elementary Education major in 1962 at Temple University. The joke on campus was that any college girl studying Elementary Ed was really going after her MRS. Degree. Her parents thought teaching was the best plan for the girl's future. She really wanted to be a writer.

The young woman's life was mapped out by her parents, by the Northeast Philadelphia Jewish community in which she grew up, and, of course by Doris Day and Donna Reed.

An aside: She had no interest in anything athletic, except her hometown sports teams. She was forever being told she was terrible at sports...and she believed the words she heard. Her classmates laughed when she had to run during gym. She was always chosen last for neighborhood pick-up games of any kind. She dreaded gym the way most kids dread calculus.

All proceeded according to plan--engaged in her senior year of college, married a month after she graduated, taught school, pregnant, first child, second child...Stop!

Here's where life's plan, as arranged by everyone but the young woman involved, had a mid-course correction, thanks to the Running Boom of the 1970s that non-athletic Donna Reed wannabe is now an athletic independent woman of—wow—70. She has developed into the person I've become.

Running has given me the opportunity to explore my limits, to test my body, and to push myself. My running roots are planted in the first Boom. They've grown deeper and stronger over the years.

Through running I experienced the joy of my body in motion; I felt the sweat drip and reveled in it. It's a cleansing, cathartic experience. I learned courage; courage to take risks, both in races and in life.

My runs give me time to connect with friends or time for some much-needed solitude. I look in the mirror and say to myself, Look at me. I'm strong. I'm fit. I'm ready for anything I'm on the verge of a different kind of marathon which will take place on May 23. The life mapped out by my parents included going to Hebrew School and studying to become a bat mitzvah at the age of 12. That was one stop on my parents' map that I chose not to visit. My parents were disappointed, but didn't push me.

Fast forward to maybe 10 years ago. My parents were gone and the thought of a bat mitzvah played in my mind. Until last summer. That's when I began my "marathon." This one, though, was about taking the first step—learning Hebrew, one letter and vowel at a time. It was as scary as committing to running 26.2 miles.

I can now see the finish line. I've learned the Hebrew alphabet (aleph-bet), the vowels, and the prayers I need to know. I'm now working on my Torah portion and Haftorah (accompanying reading).

It's been difficult at times. I became frustrated when I stumbled or forgot the letters or vowels, and when I lost focus. Then there were the times I would read the prayers almost perfectly. My rabbi and teacher, Serena Fujita, a dear friend, has been understanding and patient. We meet once a week. I study almost every day.

Anxiety and excitement—I felt that for my first marathon in 1983. I'm now preparing for a different kind of marathon. There's a saying that when a boy becomes a bar mitzvah at 13, he becomes a man ("Today I am a man") in the Jewish tradition. When I finish my "Bat Mitzvah Marathon," I'll become a woman...at 70. I hope I get a fountain pen (the traditional gift). I'll fill it with teal ink to match the streak in my hair.

A Sparkling Mom-Daughter Run

Dear Marcy,

We had no idea if we'd be able to do a mom-daughter run this year. We didn't even know if you'd be running at all. Your knee managed to keep you off the roads for the first few months of the year. Thankfully, you didn't need knee surgery.

With that burst of confidence, we sealed our mom-daughter pact. But it was not to be the Nittany Valley-Half-Marathon again this year. We focused on a different race shorter, but not easier. We were going to enter the Run for the Diamonds in Berwick on Thanksgiving Day. "Berrick" as we say in Central PA, is steeped in tradition and glory. We'd be running the same route as Johnny Kelly, Browning Ross, and Pete Pfitzinger.

I kept reminding you about "the hill." I made it sound like a cross between Mt. Everest and Pike's Peak. I wanted you to respect the course.

We woke up to rain on Thanksgiving Day. And each of us was wondering why we had ever planned to make this nine-mile race our 1998 signature event. We didn't pump each other up. Instead, we questioned our decision. But when we got to Berwick, the rain stopped and our spirits lifted. Connecting with friends, chatting about other races, feeling the energy pumped us up. By the time we got to the starting line, we were rarin' to go.

They say the third time is the charm. It may be a tired cliché, but we indeed had a charmed run. We were upbeat and happy. We chatted and laughed. And when the hill loomed in front of us, we accepted the challenge with determination and concentration. Funny that you thought the hill "wasn't so bad." Part of Mom's plan was to have you respect the hill, but not be daunted by it. Once we crested the hill, we stopped to hug and enjoy the moment this mom-daughter team was on top of the world.

We clicked off mile after mile and couldn't understand why the miles were going by so fast. Was it the cheering crowds yelling, "You go, girls;" was it the fact that we didn't take this run for granted for we knew it almost didn't happen; was it our living in the moment and letting the experience wash over us? You told me that you felt chills as we ran through the crowds and heard the cheers. This was your first race where people lined the streets. The citizens of Berwick revel in this annual event. It's as much a part of their Thanksgiving as eating turkey.

We heard Vince Wojnar announce our names as we crossed the finish line. We hugged, we smiled, we felt the joy of another mom-daughter experience. We were flying high as we made our way to the Hall. We had beaten our predicted time by eight minutes, without pushing ourselves. I guess you could say our [tired] feet didn't touch the ground.

'Muse-ings'...

My muse returned and whispered to me. "Get the words on paper. It's time."

The gentle nudge of my Muse caused a jumble of ideas to tumble around in my head. Where to begin? Running's new meaning...my winter burnout...spring's delay (the tree frogs aren't making a peep; they're probably still sleeping)...so many ideas.

Spring? What spring? Okay, Muse, I won't be coy. I'll just say it: Spring is taking her good old time to finally get to Central PA and stay. Why?...Why does winter linger like a foul smell and sweet-smelling spring seems to fly by?

Mostly it's been cold, with an icy wind, some rain, and lots of heavy overcast. Maybe it's like this every year. I get hungrier for warm sunny weather and all the lovely things that come with it as the years pass. Trying to get myself out the door to run takes every ounce of will power. My steps are heavy, my mood is heavier, and then it begins to drizzle; a cold light rain making me not only cold, but also wet. Spring's tease has become winter's joke.

But, on those days when spring does decide to tease us with sunny mild weather, I feel reborn. Soon spring's tease will become a reality. And when I hear the tree frogs, I'll know for sure.

Those of us who started running in the '70s, entered races because we loved to race, to test ourselves, to see if we could set a PR, or to see if we could beat an age-group rival. That was what running was all about. No one would wear a T-shirt that had sponsors listed all over it. Racing was about...racing.

That's changed. Racing, according to a young woman I was speaking with, is about charities.

I tried to give her a history lesson about running and to let her know that racing is mainly about testing yourself; some people do run for a charity, but racing is about racing. Running in a race means different things to different people, especially given that most races are held for a charity. But runners came first. Then charities found that races could be like the goose and the golden egg; runners being the goose and entry fees and sponsors being the...you get the idea.

I enter a new age group at the end of this year. I'll be 65 in

December. I'll always be 18 in my heart and soul and that's really what's important. No Botox, no facelift, no enhancements, or reductions. I reflect the life I've lived and, despite the "battle scars," I still see an 18-year-old girl when I look in the mirror.

Okay, Muse, I think we're finished.

It's not 'American Bandstand'

I grew up in Philly and I began watching Bandstand when Bob Horn was the host in the early '50s. When Horn was asked to leave, WFIL pulled Dick Clark—"America's Oldest Living Teenager"-- from their radio side and made him host.

The show was local--I watched every day after school, learning to dance using the banister in the living room. We all wanted to be like the "regulars"—Justine and Bob, Dotty Horner, Jimmy Peatross, Joan Buck, Big and Little Ro, Pat Molietieri, etc.

I was on Bandstand between 1957-59. I'd go with my friends. We'd "leave school early," take a bus, the el/subway, and get to 46th and Market Sts in West Philly where the WFIL studio was located, and stand in line and hope to get in. The first time I was on Bandstand I was in a teenage trance. There was Dick Clark getting things set up, talking with his producer, Tony Mammarella.

All we wanted to do was dance. We loved the rate-a-record spot and the famous "It's got a good beat, you can dance to it. I give it a 98" was part of our vocabulary.

We danced the jitterbug, Bunny Hop, the Strand, the Stomp, the South Philly Slop, the Birdland, the Cha-lypso, and more. Philly teens on Bandstand set the trends for the US once it went national in 1957.

There was a local half-hour before the national feed began. We felt that was "our time." The music was more local (doo-wop, local groups).

So many groups and singers got their start on Bandstand--Philly guys Danny and Juniors, Frankie Avalon, Fabian, Chubby Checker, Jimmy Darren, Bobby Rydell, and the Dovells...Bandstand was a must for any Rock and Roll group that wanted exposure.

I was on Bandstand one afternoon in 1959 with my friends and Dick Clark invited everyone back the following week for a night taping, something rare way back then. We went back for the taping and got to see ourselves on TV a few days later. What a thrill! What "advanced" technology! And the TV audience had no idea they were watching a taped show. I was part of an "Inside Bandstand" secret. Locals never said "American Bandstand after the show went national." It was Bandstand. Period. To us, there was no life outside of Philly.

'Turn Around'

We feel in control of our life when it's mostly predictable: family, work, running, social activities…the rhythm of life. Perhaps that rhythm is more "easy listening" rather than the energizing beat of something less comfortable.

And time…so precious and so fleeting. I think about that often as I watch my grandchildren grow and change right before my eyes. I think about it when I look at photos of Marcy and Michael and remember when they were young. All the memories of going to races with them, the adventures along the way. For some reason I thought the kids would stay little forever, even when in my heart I knew they would grow up.

Time…so precious and so fleeting. I think about the folk song "Turn Around." I cry every time I hear it. "Where have they gone, my little ones, my little ones…Turn around and they're tiny, turn around and they're grown…"

The little girl running in the Valiant Trencherman Five Miler with Mom. The little boy stopping to watch a turtle during a fun run.

Now I have similar experiences with my grandson, Shaymus, and savor them even more, as I know how precious and fleeting time is.

Take the "run" we began last Friday. I didn't really get to run, but it didn't matter. Shay and I were outside together exploring and enjoying the day.

My perspective on life has changed over the years. I remember rushing through my days, enjoying the kids, but feeling like I never had an extra minute in my very full daily life.

And then I "turned around" and my life was different. I've learned to appreciate it more.

My running…I "turned around" and got slower. I'm fine with that. As long as I get out the door to pound the pavement and race once in a while, I'm happy.

LINDA MARSH

Predictable Predicaments of Parenting

BE CAREFUL WHAT YOU WISH FOR

As first time parents, Tom and I spent much time waiting impatiently for Peter to reach those 'firsts' that would make our lives as a family easier.

For example, when Peter switched from cooing to screaming within seconds, I would have given anything for him to speak to me in a language I understood. Too soon, Peter learned to communicate verbally. Those cute little 'Mommas' and 'Daddas' turned into 'No!' (And Peter always said it with an exclamation mark!) Along with the 'No!' came the 'Why?' Have you ever tried to explain to a toddler why the sun shines? Or why some of your hairs are that funny gray color? We found ourselves longing for the days we couldn't understand a word Peter said – especially when we understood perfectly but didn't like what we heard.

Walking loomed as another eagerly anticipated milestone. Peter would have independence and our aching backs would get relief. Unfortunately, Peter often exercised his newly-earned independence by racing headlong toward the cement steps of our front porch just as I headed for the kitchen. Then there were times when Peter decided to investigate the toy department in Wal-Mart while I looked at purses.

Another highly over-rated milestone is potty training. Peter learned the skill quickly and just as quickly I wished for the good old days of diapers. Nothing disturbs a quiet church service as much as a child whispering loudly, "Mommy, I have to go NOW, and I can't hold it!" Tom and I quickly discovered the location of every bathroom in every store we frequented. We also learned to add two hours to every road trip.

THE SECOND CHILD SYNDROME

Those stories about the second child getting less love and affection than the first child seemed improbable to me. I knew Tom and I would treat all our children equally. Beth, our second child, frequently reminds us that we failed.

The first example involved the Peter Rabbit comforter given to Peter. Of course I knew one does not put a comforter on a baby – he might suffocate. But when Beth came along, it somehow appeared in her crib. She loved it at once and wouldn't let me take it away (though now she claims we didn't care if SHE suffocated).

The story of Beth's name is another sore spot. When Tom and I decided to adopt a second child, we asked for another boy, and chose the name Brett for our new son. One day during the interminable wait for word of a child that would become our son, Tom, Peter, and I went shopping. We found a cute antique shop with a collection of letters used by printers in the 'old' days. I picked out a large M for our last name, then a smaller L, T, and P. Since we knew Brett would be joining us soon, I also picked out a B.

Eventually our adoption case worker called to ask if we would consider adopting a girl. It took Tom and me exactly one second to say yes.

As we drove to meet our daughter, we discussed names. None of the names we came up with appealed to both of us, so I suggested that, since we had the B already, we name our daughter something that began with a B –Beth.

Poor second-child Beth didn't even get a name of her own.

ANIMALS

"Seriously?" I stared at Tom in amazement. "You took the kids swimming, but since the pool was closed you stopped at a pet store and bought a pair of zebra finches."

Tom nodded proudly.

We tended to be menagerie-keepers so I don't know why I was so surprised.

Soon after we married, Tom agreed to let me adopt a cat. After Peter and Beth arrived, we stopped at the Humane Society 'just to look'. We took Spirit, a rescued mixed breed, home that day. After a year as a nice, normal, two-kids-one-cat-one-dog family, all things pet went a little crazy.

Peter's kindergarten class watched eggs hatch in their classroom. We adopted five of the cute little balls of fluff. Tom built a pen in Peter's room but the little balls of fluff outgrew that within a month. Thank goodness for friends who lived on a farm!

We provided a loving home for hamsters, gerbils, fish, a hermit crab from the beach, a ribbon snake, and a tortoise Tom found walking along a two-lane road. Peter discovered he could bring mice into the house if he claimed he needed them for a class project or a Boy Scout merit badge. (I can't believe I fell for that line twice!)

Beth's contribution to our collection menagerie was rats. She began with two rats, both of whom passed on much too quickly. Another pair of female rats made Beth a grandmother to six baby rats. Thank goodness for a kindly vet who took the babies home.

The all-time worst, however, were the six Madagascar hissing cockroaches Peter brought home to care for over Spring break. They were 3" long, they hissed – and they were NOT missed when Peter took them back to school.

THUNDERSTORMS

I love thunderstorms. The intensity of Mother Nature releases some of the emotions churning inside me. I love to stand at a window and watch the storm move in, moving to a safer spot at the very last moment.

I mean I USED to love standing at the window watching the storm move in. As a a role model to two young children, watching thunderstorms from behind a fragile piece of glass is not something I want them to be doing, so I must behave.

Peter and Beth do not like thunderstorms. They hear a faint rumble of thunder when the storm is still twenty miles away and immediately rush to find a parent. During the day, we curl up with a book until the storm passes. In the middle of the night, we play musical beds so both children end up sleeping with one parent while the other parent struggles to sleep in one of the empty kid's beds.

Lately, however, the storms seem to begin right at bedtime – MY bedtime. Just as I'm curling up in bed with a good book, the rumbling starts. Tom sits downstairs in a brightly lit room, watching sports on TV. Peter, having been the last to get into bed, is the first to come tip-toeing up the steps to our bedroom. He comes to the darker, quieter space. Just as he snuggles down, Beth comes in, dragging her stuffed Bunny behind her.

I put my book down, turn out the light, and pull the covers up over the three of us. Tom peeks in at the height of the storm to find us warding off the fear with a song.

EARLY WARNING SYSTEM

Beth dropped more bombs than a B52. After months complaining of stomach pain, Beth finally agreed to see the doctor. We sat on the floor playing a game when Beth laid her cards on the table, literally. "Mom, I pierced my belly button with a needle at Amy's house."

I sat speechless, seemingly calm, as my mind whirled. Suddenly the light dawned. "Is that why you didn't want to go to the doctor?" I asked.

Beth nodded.

"All those months of pain because you were afraid Dad and I would be upset?"

I remember sitting at the kitchen table the next year when Beth walked in, dropped her books on the table, and said, "I need birth control pills." Just what the mother of a beautiful 15-year-old girl wants to hear. Whatever happened to those afternoons of cookies and milk and giggling?

Calm questioning revealed that some of Beth's friends used birth control pills for medical reasons and Beth hoped they might help her as well.

Please – some warning next time!

ONE OF THOSE MOMENTS

Children's programming at the library filled many hours during our summers. Peter, Beth, and I happened to be at the library when the librarian announced the special program for the day – a herpetologist was giving a presentation on snakes. Not only did he have pictures, he brought a boa constrictor with him.

Peter jumped at the opportunity to learn more about snakes. Beth hesitated. Snakes were slimy, and slithered on the ground. I encouraged Beth to at least listen to the presentation so Peter could enjoy it.

Personally, snakes didn't even rank in my top 50 list of favorite reptiles. They were slimy! And they crawled on the ground. And if they bit you, you could die. However, I had persuaded Beth to listen, so I had to take my own medicine.

The presenter taught us many things, including how to distinguish between poisonous and non-poisonous snakes. He claimed that snakes were NOT slimy, that their skin was cool since they were cold-blooded animals.

The presenter then brought out the boa constrictor. It was 50 feet long – okay, it was only 25 feet long – and about 24" in circumference. The presenter explained that since the snake just finished eating a chicken, he was unlikely to squeeze any fresh food.

The presenter asked for volunteers to hold the snake. Peter looked at me with eagerness, Beth with hesitation. The last thing I wanted to do was touch any part of a huge snake, but I didn't want Beth afraid of snakes for the rest of her life, either. Ah, the joys of parenting! The three of us proudly helped hold the snake.

Guess what? Snakes are NOT slimy – and Beth is not afraid of them!

DONNA VITUCCI

Waxen Image

I.

He does not live here but he is God. He is a rumor, a wastrel, an idea
of the big idea, or the thought behind the Big Idea. He is round, he is
Gaia. He's neutral on the subjects of war, gender, genocide,
celebration, the nuclear issue, the suffering of the ICU baby and the
fretwork on the doctor's forehead tending to the little gipper. Yet all
he wants is praise. His part done; hey, it was a helluva job. Arms
crossed, leans back to watch, his toe dipping through a cloud—
look!—oops, gone--his interest in us not mild nor prurient; his
interest measures on no instrument, but his wrath is seismic. And still
we fish for mercy among the minnows, for his blink, or even a wink
at us, a spot of humor like mold on the leaf's underside.

II.

Microbes came, viruses too. Wasn't nothing we could hide from.
Hitched on the wind we breathed, smoking us to ashen, smoking us
to burnt, smoking us to cinder ready to drop and be ground. Preacher
said what doesn't kill us makes us stronger. Said buck up, set your
faith 'round your shoulders, give God the glory. Bullshit, you say,
Bullshit God, all fire next time. Who to be watching and sheltering
and laying hands where hands need laying? Mama's job, Mama's
position, til Mama was struck and then it's just you. You versus tree.
You versus gale. God all mighty, hepped up on flood. River taking
out the ledge and the crops, widening its banks, growing big in its
britches, sweeping itself distant from itself. Could you ride it out, sure
you could. One more catastrophe to clean up, and there's a glint even

disaster holds in its eyes that you can't look away from. Wake unto the river, unto God's grace, the microbes soaking garbage along your front road, crusting the final stair of your back porch, foundation jilted like a lover and you a long lost child. She named you Diptheria on account of her own disease. You versus what you cannot see, and praying for light to multiply in the dark.

III.

You bred and went on round the bend, left Troy like he was a city and you a raging pony. Nana was his mom in your stead, while you went seeking stupid pleasure that might well have killed you. Your fuckin hair dyed pink then blue then purple. She said you were such a pretty little girl, but who even holds memory of that once-urchin dressed as a Halloween princess? Now Troy is coming into his words, his eyes are big and blue like yours, he works them to charm the way you did. That's how you got away with it, sister, ain't it? Every time you promised Nana, or you told her no fucking way would you change for her or anybody, no, not even for Troy. It was your fucking life to live or end living. You were a colt once and you bolted on coltish legs. Sixth grade cheerleader, she has you framed on the mantle next to a Chinese lamp, the incense burner, candles that float in a water bowl, a little offering to the Mother Mary statue she bought at a yard sale down the street from Garden Apartments, where you once had a hovel. Surprised Nana had stomach to walk to that parking lot after the ambulance call. But we have so many trips forced on us; we try not to care. We learn not to care. We don't care. Troy perks up at sirens, maybe that's enough. We'll focus on teaching him emergency isn't all it's cracked up to be. Duck the attention, boy. Keep your clean act. The street's angry with dirt you want no part of. You ever hear of horses taking needles, their eyes wild and back in their heads, reading the insides of their ears as they flick away flies?

IV.

Weeping and blood wound round. One friend in the future would wipe his tears away, but how could you know this? You always were the biggest sufferer, the goat, the play on the boardwalk that everyone turned from in embarrassment. The songs they sang, you only mouthed the words, your lips colluding and eliding, changing splash to gash and what not, other dipthongs drawn out and exploded under your shaky whine.

Your faux phonics never made it past high school. And the high pitches that drive dogs mad--what was all that ruckus on the bus for? You could cause a riot alone, and more effective, with just your eye shadow brush in the bathroom.

I carved out the belly of the guitar and there are strings in my hair. Come find me in the meadow after you've stumbled down the steps and taste concrete. I can set broken bones, I can file your jagged teeth. I'll pretty you up, honest, set a wave in your dark brown tress, you only got to ask. Meanwhile mind the traffic. It wants your gold crown for its spinning wheel.

V.

Nothing more secret than Joseph's disdain for word and law and pact. Legislators be damned. At his age the policies and debts of a nation would not affect him, though the grandchildren mattered, their courses, their struggles, the way the government would manage to fuck them. Future had a different sound now. More hollow than rosy, foreshortened.

He could sit in his broke-down easy chair, broken down just the way he liked it, just the way he'd been working into it for twenty years, with the aim toward this broke-down easiness that suffused his spine, that numbed his flat ass. The chair, where he rested back to burn a few, lighting the next off the end of the last, no one warning over what he was doing to his lungs. Whistle was part of his breath.

Outside the kids bouncing their basketball in the alley gave him a heartbeat and a thread in his head that knocked blinds loose in the windows, an insistent tree limb against the window wanting to shatter. Things were hollow or they were heavy, and sometimes both. All the times his mother had exclaimed, "I don't know if I'm on foot or on horseback," he never knew what she meant, but he got it now, living at the center of a maelstrom of which he wasn't really part. The tornado had already passed and didn't deem him worth sucking up into the cloud. This was a different storm, a different earth than the one he'd been born to and lived on. No storm cellars for hiding from this kind of weather and he a shrieking lightning rod pawning off pain with a piece of church jewelry. He wrapped the rosary around his neck and crumbled two teeth biting down on the cross.

VI.

Yellow like catastrophe and the thing took hold. You'd like to think when you screw up that the bad comes from the outside, not your fault, you're in the clear. But come on now, you know your locust shell is the center of the investigation, sacrificed to the volcano-god, first to be burnt, first, second and last. That spiral of getting caught never eases up, the choke-hold on your spleen that wrings sweat from your pores until the stuff runs yellow. Yellow-bellied and still trying to shift them to some other stiff. Well, it can't all be on you, can it? You're too dumb to cross up the traffic lights the way they claim. Jailhouse Snitch is a rough nickname to suffer but it's pretty damn close. Your magnet pulls the shifting winds your way, and look, you've ransomed them again, your kin and your birthright, all the way up the tree to Cain's branch. The shell game and the quarter behind the ear ain't nothing, nor the flowing scarves from up your tattered arm. Come now. Make this bird disappear; make this rabbit turn to a hog. I got your back, Sissy. I got you back and front.

VII.

Inside my blind term resided so much clatter and clang, I might as well be in a silverware drawer. Metal on metal my connections creaked; they replaced what was replaceable, and left it to me to oil up the rest. The sidewalk stir was nothing. The limp-alongs blended in with the gross and the dreaded, better if you clamped your jaws shut. No teeth to grit. I sucked the songs my mam sang me through a bowl in my head, that everlasting loop from gums to back of the throat, roof of the mouth all spit. Music a charm, music carry should you allow it, throw you back to the shore of Gun Lake and your childhood-self digging into the side of a sand bluff. Wonder it didn't collapse, but then I thought that's just how a miner'd of felt on a cave-in and me aching to know what Daddy last visioned before summoning the Lord and gaining the Devil. Fled Coal City, my own self a flatbed a'froth atop the river. Downstream gotta be better. Ever the southern parts calling, a witch-spell about my bones, drawing blood to the surface, justifying pain for a price, and I coughed up my last on some fool's promise. I sure am hungry, starving more than thirsty, and sizing up your pockets so I start me a'hummin', and you can't look nowhere else, see?

PAMELA VARKONY

We Live

Chandra and Chakras

The bulletin board at our "over 55" community contained the usual white, 3x5 index card offerings, furniture, cars, massage. Standing out in rainbow colors was a flyer for a "Metaphysical Expo:" Too tempting an invitation for a 60's flower child to resist.

The day of the event, the parking lot of the community center was packed...not a space to be had. Row after row of golf carts and four-door sedans stood as testament to the lure of the unknown.

Whatever needs your heart and soul might have, and looking at the crowd, those needs were many, a solution was only a tarot card, palm reading, or psychic interpretation away. Should words be too transient, take comfort home by purchasing angels in all shapes and sizes, crystals in specific colors to open and balance your chakras...the seven places in your body where energy flows in and out. Your meditations or lamentations could be guided by mantras printed on parchment. Chandra, a psychic reader, seemed to be particularly popular with a long waiting list. The white board described her skills as "a true messenger of the Spirit for those seeking to connect to loved ones who have crossed over to the other side." Her other talents included Balancing of Chakras, Shamanism and Manifestation of our Desires. I admit, that "manifestation of my desire" thing sounded appealing.

Feeling I should contribute to the general welfare since admission was free, I purchased lavender scented, holistically made, goat's milk soap. I stopped to talk to a smiling Asian woman who was doing Acupuncture. She offered to give me a quick demonstration. The incense in the air must have gotten to me because I allowed this perfect stranger, sitting on a stool beside a card table, to insert two steel needles into my ears.

The power of the mind is a wonderful thing: Five minutes later the needles were removed and I swear I felt better…lighter, almost like my head was floating. Luckily it was still attached as were my ears. It occurred to me that I might be about to faint so I sat down. I didn't faint, but I did feel "different."

My needle induced euphoria was short lived. I was nearly knocked down by a woman who was sobbing as she walked away from a reading with Chandra, mumbling, "I knew he would wait for me."

Karma

She smiled at me as I walked past her car
Sitting there staring through the windshield
Her silver hair barely visible over the steering wheel
From behind me I heard a soft voice say
"Beautiful day isn't it, I hope you don't mind"
I turned and smiled, "Yes it is" I replied
She looked as though she did not hear
So I added, "A rare gift for this time of year"
As I approached my car, she stepped outside
Asking "Where did you have your lunch?"
Saying again, "I hope you don't mind"
The question seemed not to be about a reply
As it was about finding a direction
I offered a thought about a place she might enjoy
Opened my door, then said goodbye
As I turned the key I heard her say
"I just had to get out of the house today"
I will always regret driving away
Leaving her behind
One day I may be the elder stranger
Needing someone to be patient and kind
Desperate for the warmth of another soul
For no other reason than I've grown old
If fate and karma provide the chance
Next time I'll give more than a passing glance

Mirror Mirror on the Wall

So many things my mother told me would happen have happened. I wish I had learned to play the piano; paid more attention in Spanish class; and saved more money.

Of all the wisdom she imparted what continues to resonate is how hard it would be to watch my youth disappear. "You never think it's going to be you," she said. "When you're young, you're convinced you can beat the game."

I remember walking past her slightly open bedroom door seeing her staring in the mirror running her hands over her face. I'd never seen her look so sad...or defeated. Father Time was winning the game. She was in her late fifties.

Since then, science and surgery have stepped in to level the field upon which Father Time marches: In my mother's day, people in their 60's and 70"'s were considered "old." Now, popular culture is full of references to 60 being the new 40. A charming, reassuring thought, however from personal experience I can tell you, sixty is nothing like 40...except in my head, where I am frozen at 35.

The closer we are to each end of life, the more compressed the differences. There's a big difference in size, strength, and ability between a child of five and a child of ten, yet there's almost no perceptible difference between an adult of 40 and one of 45. At the other end of the journey, the process is reversed: At 60, I traveled to Afghanistan as a writer and women's advocate. At 65, recovering from a hip replacement, I would not have attempted such an adventure.

Fully recovered I'm once again taking regular trips to the gym, using the most hi-tech creams and potions I can afford and enduring the occasional injection of deadened plague. That 35 year old who lives in my head remains game for anything.

As I told my children during my last birthday celebration, "I'm not going down without a fight."

Side by Side

When we were five
We sat side by side in your back yard

On a picnic bench under a tree
We played and laughed till we fell on the ground
Life was all about you and me

When we were twenty-five
We were a couple of brides
Making our dreams come true
We were young and thin: Trying to please our men
Life was all shiny and new

When we were fifty-five
We prayed side by side
As our children walked down the aisle
We dreamed of trips in the sun, grandchildren to come
Ahead, lay so many miles

And now here we are
Once again side by side
As we tearfully say our goodbye
With you being brave and me pretending its okay
Both knowing you're too young to die

This ending is not what we planned
When we walked hand in hand
Through so many of life's troubles and joys

I'll never forget the places we've been ·
The laughter, the triumphs, the fun
For me you'll always be just a memory away
Until we sit side by side again

Old Man River

As I stood beside the river, the voice in my head said, "too high, too fast, too much debris." I, along with my husband and two friends, climbed into the kayaks, anyway.

My voice quieted as we floated past blooming water lilies and sunbathing turtles. Lulled into a false sense of security by the warmth of a Florida February day, I began to take photographs.

In an instant, the view through the camera was black. Cold, dirty water swirled around me: I'm submerged. Fighting for air I make it to the surface. My husband, where is my husband? The current is so strong I can barely turn my head to get my bearings. I'm in the middle of the river, being carried downstream by the current. I have to make it to shore.

I'm pulled under for a second time. I'm trying not to panic. I hear my husband saying to our friends, save her, save her. With every ounce of strength I have I start across the current toward the bank. A lifeline...I reach a fallen tree and although I'm not on land I have something to hang on to.

Searching, I see my husband in the river, tangled in trees and brush, fighting to get free. Our friends, inexperienced kayakers, are helpless to rescue us.

After what felt like hours, we both miraculously end up on the bank, barely breathing, covered in mud. Lying fifty feet away we turn to see the other and as our eyes meet, we start to laugh uncontrollably. We live.

NICHOLAS DIGIOVANNI

Man Has Premonition of Own Death

A Look of Agony

I've seen autopsy photos. I know people often die with their eyes open and that their eyes may stay open until someone gently shuts them. I don't know the science of this, but I gather that the eyelids of the dead tend to pop back open after you close them, hence the old practice of placing heavy coins upon the eyes. Nowadays, I gather, the eyes are sewn or glued. And so the dead look like they're sleeping, although if you look closely you soon realize that it's a weird, disconcerting sleep, the deepest sleep, a sleep in which the eyes never move and twitch, in which there is no dreaming soul behind the eyes.

Emily Dickinson wrote:

I like a look of Agony, Because I know it's true —

Emily was on the right track. Let's not shut the eyes of the dead. Let's look death straight in the eye.

Don't Fear the Reaper?

About ten years ago, I looked death straight in the eye. No, wait, that sounds much too much like a line from a Clint Eastwood or John Wayne movie. Let me rephrase that: Nearly ten years ago, I nearly died.

I was in my early 50s. I had a blocked artery—the result, the cardiologist later told me, of 35 years of smoking cigarettes. The details of what happened next are relatively boring: A stent was inserted into the blocked artery, I stayed in the hospital for a few days, quit smoking, went to cardiac rehabilitation for six weeks, took my meds regularly and religiously, and I've been pretty much OK since then.

Except I still remember what it felt like. It wasn't anything dramatic. It just made me sad. I thought "Is that all it is?" I felt like I was slowly fading away....like someone had pulled a plug...I really and truly could feel my energy—my life—seeping slowly from my body. And the overwhelming, overriding feeling? It wasn't fear. It wasn't any sense of regret. It was just a deep melancholy, as I realized that life, goddamn, after all the sound and fury, after all the power and glory, after all the snap, crackle and pop, simply slips away.

No Joke

When I was young, I joked about death. I told a few people what I wanted done at my funeral: I suggested that the room be kept nearly dark, lit by a few flickering candles. As the weeping mourners entered the room, a spotlight would suddenly switch on and illuminate a comfortable chair, where my still young and beautiful corpse would be sitting up, supported by pillows, with wires attached to my head, arms and legs. Push a button: I cross my left leg casually across my right. Push another: My arm raises a cigarette to my mouth, which has been fixed by the mortician into a bemused grin. Push a third button: My head tilts ever so slightly. Push the button that says SOUND and a prerecorded tape plays the sound of my voice saying "I'd like to welcome you all to my funeral!"

At this point, I imagined, screams and hysteria and sobs would erupt, while I sat there silently surveying the scene.

No Joke (Part Two)

When I was in my twenties, you see, death was a concept, not real, something that happened to people when they grew old — which I, of course, wouldn't. But somewhere, somehow, something clicked inside my brain and said: "Hey, wake up. You're going to die. All of your friends are going to die. Your whole family is going to die. You know when you drive down the street? All those people you see in all of those cars? Every one of them is going to die. Every single person you've ever encountered. Everyone you've ever known. Everyone you've ever glimpsed. Everyone. And there's nothing you can do about it."

I've been accused of being death-obsessed. But I am not morbid. I just want to live forever.

Man Has Premonition of Own Death (Part One)

When I return to my hometown of Yonkers, New York, an old industrial city on the Hudson River, I always make sure I drive past the former Alexander Smith carpet mills and the nearby Oakland Cemetery. If I leave the windows open, I might hear the sound of a sudden splash, of shouts of alarm, of agonized screams, as my great-uncle Thomas Crooks, 23 years old, tumbles into a vat of acid used to cure carpet fabrics at the mill.

The year is 1928. His co-workers pull Thomas out of the vat, wrap him in burlap, and carry him to the old St. Joseph's Hospital. Others rush to the nearby home of Thomas' mother, Pauline Crooks, my great-grandmother on my mother's side. My great-grandmother arrives at the hospital and embraces her burned and dying son. His skin is red and blistered and peeling like tissue paper. Thomas dies in his mother's arms.

Next morning, the Yonkers Herald-Statesman reports on the mishap at the carpet mill. The headline reads: MAN HAS PREMONITION OF OWN DEATH. The article describes how young Thomas had met his fiancée for a picnic lunch under a tree at the Oakland Cemetery. According to the article, when the mill's whistle sounded, Thomas started to return to work. But "before returning to work, Mr. Crooks turned to her and said, 'I am going in. But I shall be carried out.' " Fifteen minutes later came my ancestor's fateful plunge into that acid bath.

The newspaper article goes on to describe my great-grandmother's arrival at the hospital, just in time for her young son's death. This is the last sentence of the article: "Mrs. Crooks was burned about the face as she continually kissed her dying son."

My mother remembers that her Grandma Crooks had tiny scars all around her lips. She'd never known how her grandmother had acquired those scars. "They weren't really scars," I say. "They were birthmarks."

Man Has Premonition of Own Death (Part Two)

Yes, ghosts are everywhere in my hometown. They stroll down the old streets carrying parasols. They drive fast cars past the strip malls along Central Avenue. They sit in the grandstands and watch the sulkies at the old Empire Racetrack. They haunt each and every one of Yonkers' seven hills—including the tree-covered Oakland Cemetery. It's still there, still hauntingly beautiful, with narrow curving lanes winding around fading gravestones and mossy monuments. It would still be a good place to have a picnic lunch with your girlfriend. I sometimes drive to the top of the hill there, sit in my car, and drink my morning coffee.

My maternal great-grandparents and grandparents are all buried at Oakland Cemetery. So are two victims of the sinking of the Titanic, Alexander and Charity Robins. And so is a Yonkers physician named Dr. Charles Leale, who just happened to be working in Washington for the government in 1865 when John Wilkes Booth just happened to shoot and kill Abraham Lincoln. Leale was the first doctor to arrive at the side of the mortally wounded president, and he took charge of the initial efforts to save Lincoln's life.

The grave of Dr. Leale is located within shouting distance of the grave of Thomas Crooks, who abides in the Crooks family plot a few hundred feet from the wrought-iron gates of the cemetery. I hope Dr. Leale's black bag contains a soothing salve that heals my poor ancestor's scars and helps to ease his sorrow.

Days of Our Lives

We were driving around a lovely island in Rhode Island's Narragansett Bay when we decided to walk down the rocks to the water. We headed slowly toward the crashing waves, careful about where we stepped, wary of falling and getting hurt on the rocks. And then I slipped. My feet flew out from under me and I was sliding down an incline. My companion shouted my name. And suddenly I was underwater. My head made contact with a smooth rock—the impact, luckily, cushioned by the water.

I popped up in a deep narrow crevice that had been carved out of the rock by the waves, standing on slippery rocks in water that was about chest-high. The ledge I'd fallen off was at least two feet above my head. I could reach it by stretching my arms upward, but the rock was slippery and there was nothing to grab hold of.

I squeezed through a narrow passageway, moving about six feet in the direction of the shore, toward the water. If I could get through there, I might be about to pull myself up onto the somewhat lower ledge. I squeezed through sideways. Then I pulled myself, bracing my legs again one rock wall while boosting my body up onto a flat rock on the other side, then rolling onto my stomach and crawling up to a drier, safer rock.

As I walked carefully up the rocks, checking to make certain I hadn't broken any bones or cut the back of my head, I had an image of the opening credits of an old TV soap opera. There was a close-up of an hourglass and a narrator's voice declaring ominously and with great authority: "Like sands in an hourglass…These are the days of our lives…"

Life Is Hell (Part One)

My father was an upbeat kid. Second-generation Italian, son of immigrants, grew up during World War II listening dreamily to radio shows that transported him from his tiny tenement apartment in Yonkers to places around the world, dreamed big romantic dreams and believed they could come true. Wanted to be an architect!

By the time he was in his late thirties he was grossly overweight and knew his dreams were not coming true, and he somehow reached his fifties when years of eating lots and lots of what's bad for your health led to a massive heart attack and a 10-year gradual decline that ended when my father was found unconscious on the floor of his hospital bathroom, slipped into an irreversible coma, then breathed his last breath just minutes after my family decided to take the doctor's advice and end life support.

Did I mention that my father, somewhere along the line, decided—or figured out—that Earth was actually Purgatory?

Life Is Hell (Part Two)

The Roman Catholic Church defines purgatory as a sort of holding cell—a place where sinners go to be purged of sin and are eventually allowed to enter heaven. It may not be an actual place—it may be more like a state of existence. And the real punishment and pain, at least this is the way I understood it when I was a kid, was in the knowledge that heaven was oh-so-close but yet so far, the overwhelming sorrow and frustration of not yet being able to gaze upon the face of God.

Here's an interesting aside. We all think of Hell as a place where we burn for eternity, right? Why's the Devil red? Because he's got the worst sunburn ever, right? Wrong. St. Thomas Aquinas—pardon me, but I still haven't completely freed myself from the chains of 14 years of Catholic school education—said flames are used only in Purgatory, as a cleansing device.

Go to Hell, and the torture is more varied, more creative: worms, horrible heat, ungodly thirst, horrid screams, eternal dismemberment, and…you get the idea.

But wait! It gets more confusing. I read somewhere that St. Augustine suspected that God, in all his glorious Economy, used the very same fires in Hell and Purgatory, but for different purposes.

Augustine and Aquinas both suggested, then, that Hell and Purgatory might be adjacent to each other. Sort of like driving through a bad neighborhood into one that's even worse.

Life Is Hell (Part Three)

One of Martin Luther's biggest gripes was the sale and purchase of "indulgences," which were—and are—specific amounts of "time off" granted to sinners sent to Purgatory. There are still prayer cards that specify how many days off their punishment may be granted to a soul in Purgatory if the prayer prays this prayer for the unfortunate departed. The Catholic Church's All Souls Day, two days after Halloween, is a day devoted entirely to prayers aimed at easing the pain of Purgatory.

Ever hear or read about the hell hole discovered by scientists–and kept secret until it was revealed in an expose published in *Weekly World News*? Scientists drilling to study the earth's deep core thought they heard noise coming up through the hole. When they lowered microphones into the hole, the scientists realized that the sounds were actually the awful anguished cries of souls burning in Hell! The scientists quickly filled in the hole, but not before a fiery figure rose from the hole, scared the crap out of the scientists and ordered them to cap the well.

My poor father just might have believed this story. Or he might have agreed with the members of an obscure sect called the Unity School of Christianity, who believe Heaven resides inside us all. Likewise, they don't believe Hell and Purgatory are actual places—instead, they are nothing more than a state of mind, the realm of mental and emotional anguish, the place in our hearts and minds and souls where sorrow and sadness abide. Maybe this was what my father meant. I find some comfort in thinking that perhaps Death brought my father blessed relief.

Huckleberry Friends

News of the death of Andy Williams made me think of my father, who loved "Moon River," which was written by Henry Mancini for the movie "Breakfast at Tiffany's" and was a hit record in at least two versions that I know of: an instrumental by Mantovani and His Orchestra and the vocal rendition by Williams.

My father and his friends, all children of Italian immigrants, attached great value to certain things they perceived as emblems of American affluence. My father, for instance, bought golf clubs and went through a phase of playing on Saturdays at the local public links, but then gave it up—I believe because he was too tired from working two and sometimes three jobs. Likewise, he had a bar in his living room where he made highballs and whiskey sours for his friends and aspired to have a finished basement with a really nice hi-fi system where he could listen to Mantovani and Streisand and Sinatra and Perry Como...and Andy Williams, with his mohair sweaters and winning smile.

"Moon River," with its romance and its nostalgia and beautiful air of melancholy and longing, moves me whenever I hear it, for I can hear my father singing along to the instrumental version by Mantovani. "Moon River" reminds me of cool autumn nights with their whisper of winter to come. The song also makes me think of a young man in the late springtime of his life—my father would have been in his early 30s during those years—who still believed his dreams could and would come true, "just around the bend," for himself and his "huckleberry friends."

Getting in the Last Word

What words would you choose to utter if you knew they would be the final words you spoke in this mortal realm?

Novelist Victor Hugo declared, "I see black light," which isn't encouraging. Thomas Edison, on the other hand, reported: "It is very beautiful over there." The very first Queen Elizabeth tried to cut a deal when her time came in the early 1600s: "All my possessions for a moment of time."

The film producer Louis B. Mayer, declared on his deathbed, "Nothing matters. Nothing matters." Let's add James Joyce to this gloomy mix. The great writer died with this question unanswered: "Does nobody understand?" And, OK, we might as well mix some doom into the gloom...Edgar Allan Poe's final plea: "Lord help my poor soul." You think the great Henry David Thoreau had something profound to say when he heard the Grim Reaper's knock? Nope. Henry's last utterance: "Moose...Indian..."

I like poet Emily Dickinson's farewell: "I must go in, the fog is rising." But this may be my favorite. President James K. Polk, when he died in 1849, told first lady Sarah Polk: "I love you Sarah. For all eternity, I love you."

That's what I want—I want my heart's true fulfillment right there by my side, close enough for her to hear me whisper those three perfect words: "I love you."

ABOUT THE AUTHORS

Tomas Benitez

Tomas Benitez was born and raised in front of a TV set in East LA. He has been an arts and cultural advocate for nearly forty years. As a writer he has written films (SALSA, Cannon Films, 1987) and theatre, as well as fiction, poetry and television. He is a freelance proposal writer and cultural commentator. He is Chairman of the Board of the Latino Arts Network, and is a former commissioner with the County of Los Angeles Arts Commission. He is a contributing writer and founding member of the Baseball Reliquary's Latino Baseball History Project, a study of the Latino experience in America through the lens of baseball. He continues to live in East Los Angeles with Jinx, a cat who thinks he's a dog.

G. Bruce Boyer

G. Bruce Boyer has been a noted men's fashion writer and editor for more than forty years. He was associated with *Town & Country* magazine as Men's Fashion Editor for fifteen years. His feature articles have also appeared in *Esquire, Harper's Bazaar, Forbes, The New York Times, The New Yorker, Departures,* and *The Rake* among other national and international magazines. He was the first American fashion journalist to write for the noted Italian fashion magazine *L'Uomo Vogue* .

He is the author of two books on the history and direction of men's fashion: *Elegance* (W. W. Norton & Company, New York, 1985); *Eminently Suitable* (W. W. Norton & Company, New York, 1990). Additionally, he is the author of two books on the history of fashion in the cinema: *Rebel Style: Cinematic Heroes of the Fifties* (Assouline Press, 2006), and *Fred Astaire Style* (Assouline Press, 2005). He is a co-author of a three-volume study of American menswear in the 1930s, entitled *Apparel Arts* (Gruppo GFT, Milan, 1989), and a contributor and consultant to *The Encyclopedia of Clothing and Fashion* (Charles' Scribners' Sons, 2004). He co-authored *Gary Cooper: Enduring Style* (PowerHouse Books, 2011) with Mr. Cooper's daughter Maria Cooper Janis.

He has appeared on national TV, National Public Radio, and as consultant and commentator on the TV documentary series for American Movie Classics, The Hollywood Fashion Machine.

Most recently he has been associated with several exhibitions at The Museum at The Fashion Institute of Technology. In 2013 he was asked to co-curate the Ivy Style exhibit and contributed to the accompanying book published by Yale University Press. Along with Patricia Mears, Deputy Director of The Museum, he also co-curated the exhibition *Elegance in an Age of Crisis: Fashions of the 1930s* in 2014, and co-authored the accompanying book published by Yale UP.

He has been coordinator of public relations and media for the Custom Tailors & Designers Association of America, and is an editorial consultant on clothing, fashion, and grooming. His extensive knowledge of the clothing industry and custom trades has also led him to private and corporate image consulting, and writer/consultant to the clothing manufacturing industry, designers, and retailers. He has produced public relations, promotional text material, and advertising for Paul Stuart, Zegna, Brioni, Faconnable, Loro Piana, Kiton, Borrelli, Robert Tallbot, Edward Green, Polo/ Ralph Lauren, Bergdorf Goodman, Drake's of London, Gant, Joseph Abboud, and Vitale Barberis Canonico, among other international firms.

His latest book, *True Style: the History & Principles of Classic Menswear*, was published by Basic Books in September, 2015. He is currently working on a study of menswear in the 1950s, titled *All Shook Up: Men's Fashion in a Postwar Culture.*

Jim Brega

Jim Brega earned his BA from San Diego State University and an MFA from the University of Illinois. His work has appeared in a number of journals and anthologies, including, among others, *Lunch Ticket, Lime Hawk, Hippocampus Magazine, Red Savina Review, Plenitude, r.kv.r.y.*, and the anthologies *The Best of Foliate Oak* (2012) and *A Year in Ink 5*. He has crossed the US by car six times, and believes there's only one way to appreciate the vastness of America, the spirit and resolution of her people, the beauty and variety of her geography. You must be on the ground. You must be willing to drive. You must travel her.

Jim lives near San Diego with his spouse, the artist and writer John Castell. You can find more of Jim's work on his blog, www.jimbrega.com.

Nancy Canyon

Nancy Canyon's prose & poetry is published in *Water~Stone Review, Fourth Genre, Floating Bridge Review, Able Muse, Poetry South, Main Street Rag, Exhibition, Obliquity, Labyrinth, Sue C. Boynton, Clover: A Literary Rag,* and more. Ms. Canyon holds the MFA in Creative Writing from Pacific Lutheran University. She's a creative writing instructor for Whatcom Community College and visual artist. Her eBook "Dark Forest" can be found at Amazon.com. "Saltwater" a book of poetry can be purchased at www.villagebooks.com. She keeps an art studio in the Morgan Block Studios in Historic Fairhaven. www.nancycanyon.com

Freddi Tachman Carlip

Freddi was born in South Philadelphia and grew up in Northeast Philly. She graduated from Temple University with a degree in Elementary Education. Writing has always been her first love.

Running gave Freddi the wings she needed. Freddi was a pioneer in women's running. She took her first running steps in 1978 and has never stopped.

In 1981 Freddi purchased *Runner's Gazette*, America's first running newspaper, and became its editor/ publisher, while using a Compugraphic typesetting machine.

In 1994 Freddi became Eastern Director of the Road Runners Club of America and in 2000 was elected its third woman president. During her tenure, she acted as publisher of *Boom! 40 Years of Running and Writing* for the RRCA and developed her alter ego, Miss Road Manners, to help new runners learn the etiquette of running.

Poetry has always been a vital part of Freddi's life. She's composed poems while running, while traveling, and during life changes that sparked her muse. She led a local poetry group for five years.

Freddi's travels have taken her throughout the United States, the Caribbean, Great Britain, Kenya, Israel, and South Korea. She loves to travel, experience life as it comes, watch classic movies, dance, watch her Philly sports teams, listen to music, and read. She finds peace and contentment enjoying the wildlife at her home.

Freddi writes a social column for the local paper and covers events throughout the area. Her publisher dubbed her the "Hedda Hopper of the Susquehanna Valley."

Freddi celebrated her bat mitzvah at age 70 after studying with her rabbi for almost a year.

Freddi lives in Lewisburg, PA with her four cats, two dogs, and her guy. She has two children and two grandchildren. Freddi continues to write, to dance, to laugh, and to follow her muse.

Tom Carter

Tom Carter is an outdoor enthusiast, a professor, and an executive in a revolutionary clean energy firm. He is an avid cyclist, trail runner, hiker, open-water swimmer, and animal lover. He is the Vice President of

Government Affairs at Blue Planet, Ltd, which is developing processes to turn carbon emissions into concrete. He teaches classes on various environmental issues at both George Mason University and at the University of Maryland. He also teaches rock climbing and is certified as a facilitator in outdoor challenge course. Tom also loves travel, film, and music. While earning his Juris Doctor degree from the University of North Carolina, he founded a music management company and record label and toured extensively with an indie rock band.

Nicholas DiGiovanni

Nicholas DiGiovanni is a novelist, essayist, award-winning journalist, blogger and teacher of creative writing. His novella "Rip," a modern-day parody of Washington Irving's "Rip Van Winkle," was published in 2011 by Black Angel Press. His fiction has appeared in *Paterson Literary Review*, *Identity Theory*, *The Caribbean Writer*, and elsewhere. He has been the recipient of five fiction-writing fellowships at the prestigious Virginia Center for the Creative Arts. DiGiovanni founded the Delaware Valley Poetry Festival, held annually in western New Jersey from the late 1990s through the late 2000s, which featured many widely-acclaimed poets including former U.S. poets laureate Robert Pinsky, Rita Dove and Louise Gluck and Pulitzer Prize winner Paul Muldoon. He grew up in Yonkers, N.Y., and currently lives in Highland Park, N.J. His website, "World of Wonders," can be found at www.nicholasgiovanni.com.

Susan Lee Feathers

Susan Lee Feathers received a B.A. in American Literature from East Tennessee State University and a Master's Degree in Special Education from the University of Tennessee. Susan devoted the first 15 years of her professional life to teaching English and Life Sciences, and another 10 years in environmental education. Her nonfiction publications include: Paean to the Earth (2008); SEJ Journal of the Society of Environmental Journalists, Hope Beneath Our Feet (2011) an anthology of essays edited by Martin Keogh and published by North Atlantic Press, and travel articles in Pensacola Magazine (2010-11), and Panoply Zine (2015). Susan's blog, WalkEarth.org has published her nonfiction and fiction works since 2009. Susan resides in Pensacola, Florida where she writes, supports businesses through Susan Feathers Associates, and enjoys living on the Gulf. Susan writes about humans and nature. Threshold, her first novel, will be published in 2016. It focuses on climate change in the Southwestern U.S.

Mary Flood

Mary Flood is a blogger and observer of the absurd. Growing up as the eighth of eleven children, she discovered early on that the way to be heard among all the babble was to speak softly, but even then she had a lot to say that was lost in the chorus surrounding her. Now through her writing she raises her voice and is heard among the din. Mary lives in Connecticut in her childhood home where she is busy encouraging the walls to talk. Follow her at https://ramblingonline.wordpress.com

Victoria Franzese

Victoria Franzese is a fierce New Yorker who worked for many years as a marketing executive in the financial and information services industries. Then she owned, operated, and wrote for a profitable and critically acclaimed online travel guide, ultimately selling it to a major media outlet after fifteen years. Now, thankfully, she can write on a variety of different topics and all of her travel is purely for fun. She is a contributing writer for BuzzFeed, Imaginate magazine, and Mapquest. She also does freelance writing for a number of corporate clients.

Victoria is a graduate of Smith College and New York University's Leonard N. Stern School of Business. She lives with her darling husband, two strong-willed and opinionated teenage sons, and a sweet Goldendoodle named Jenkins.

Peter W. Fong

Peter W. Fong is the author of the award-winning novel, *Principles of Navigation*, a love story set in the Florida Keys. His work has appeared in *American Fiction, Gray's Sporting Journal, the New York Times Sophisticated Traveler*, and many other magazines and anthologies. He lives in Tangier, Morocco.

Paul Heller

Fortunate by birth and circumstance. Magna Cum Laude at an elite private school. Graduated from an Ivy League college. Two weeks after graduating, ran for it. Spent the next 5 years working on shrimp boats, oil exploration boats, partnered a shipyard. Lost a virgin wife to a virus. Afterwards, a decade itinerant in Maine and Spain and Third Avenue barrooms. Has been almost everywhere. Done almost everything. Worships the Enlightenment. Heller is the author of the #1 Kindle bestseller, *Last Call: My Mother's Descent into Darkness* (Blue Heron Book Works, 2013).

Mary Lawlor

Mary Lawlor is Professor of English, Emerita, Muhlenberg College; author of *Fighter Pilot's Daughter: Growing Up in the Sixties and the Cold War* (Rowman & Littlefield paperback 2015); *Public Native America: Tribal Self-Representation in Casinos, Museums and Powwows* (Rutgers UP, 2006); and *Recalling the Wild: Naturalism and the Closing of the American West* (Rutgers UP, 2000). She lives in Allentown, PA and Gaucin, Spain.

Linda Marsh

Linda Marsh graduated from the University of Northern Colorado with a Bachelor of Arts degree in Special Education. She then taught special needs children for seven years before earning a Master's of Religious Education from the Presbyterian School of Christian Education in Richmond, VA. After marriage and a move to the mid-west, Linda taught developmentally delayed preschool children. She is currently employed as a technical writer for a telecommunications company. Linda has other published works including an American History curriculum as well as Sunday school and Bible School curricula, an adult study book on Women in the Bible, and a preschool Advent activity book. Linda and her husband Gary have a goal of seeing a game in every Major League baseball park now that their two children are grown.

Ann Sonz Matranga

Ann Sonz Matranga grew up on Long Island in the 1950s. With four well-hidden Jewish grandparents, surrounded by the anti-Semitism of the day, she was raised a Roman Catholic. Thus it may not be surprising that she writes about characters with secret identities. She graduated from Marymount Academy, Tulane University, and the Heller School at Brandeis. Ann worked for a health insurance organization where she founded a program known as SLA (Service Level Agreement, not the Symbionese Liberation Army). She raised her two children in Brookline, Mass. and in 1990, the family moved to northern California. Ann has three grandchildren who call her Bubbe, pronounced bubbie, Yiddish for grandma. For the past fifteen years she has served as developmental editor for many published authors of nonfiction and memoir. After a long hiatus, she is also working on a novel, and she's excited to have guidance from Bathsheba Monk. She says of her writing, "It's all about the secrets." Her editor's web site is www.annmatranga.com

Jonah Matranga

The centers of Jonah Matranga's heart for the last 20 years have been raising his daughter, singing, making stuff, and speaking up. He lives in San Francisco, out by Land's End, with rent control.

G.B. Miller

G. B. Miller has worked in theatre for over 40 years as an actor, director, playwright, designer and educator. He is Artistic Director of Selkie Theatre, a dual citizenship theatre based in Allentown and Galway, Ireland.

Well known for his solo shows, he considers himself a student of history and theater, creating performances and characters by commission for educational and historical organizations, including Mark Twain, General Harry C. Trexler, Asa Packer and T. S. Eliot.

New plays George has written for theatre include "Walking with Daylight" about Bethlehem's Moravian's and the Lenni Lenape; "Street People: Ghosts at the End of the Century" portraying the transparency of the homeless; and "A Moment with Nelle Harper Lee," a co-written solo show. He has served as a journalist and reporter for the *Evening Courier* and *The Times News*, and his freelance writing can be seen most recently in the *Inside Allentown* guide published annually by the Chamber of Commerce.

Judith Farmer Miller

Judith Farmer Miller was born, Feb. 19, 1931 in Brooklyn, New York. Her parents moved to Manhattan when she was a toddler. At five years old she first heard her father's "Big Band" play an afternoon gig at Rockefeller Center. Her family then moved to New Jersey where she went to public elementary school until they moved to Hillside, N.J. where she entered 4th grade and graduated from Hillside High School, continuing her education at Cedar Crest College in Allentown, PA. She worked as a Home Service Representative for the Elizabethtown Gas Co. in Elizabeth, N.J. In December of 1952 she married Morton J. Miller. Their wedding was at the Ambassador Hotel in NYC and father's band played for the reception. She has 2 grown children and 3 grandchildren.

Morton J. Miller

Morton J. Miller was born February 12, 1924 in Brooklyn, NY. He attended elementary school at the Hebrew Institute of Boro Park in Brooklyn through 9th grade. He moved to Allentown, Pa at the age of fourteen and graduated from Allentown High School in 1941. He matriculated at the University of Pennsylvania upon graduation from high school until March of 1943 when he was inducted into the Army Air Corps. He remained in the service until October of 1945 and returned to Penn in January of 1946 and graduated in June of 1947. At that time he started an apparel manufacturing business in partnership with his brother-in-law. He was married to his wife Judith in December of 1952. They have two children. He sold his interest in his business in 1990 and has been retired since then.

Gail Reitano

Gail Reitano was born and raised in the New Jersey Pine Barrens, the granddaughter of a farmer and the niece of a property developer, and her work focuses on that unique sociology and physical environment. A recently completed novel, Headfire, is about fire ecology and the fight of a lone wolf with a distrust of authority to preserve this natural treasure.

Gail's fiction has been published in London, where she lived for twelve years. She won a short story prize from *Glimmer Train Press*, and her work was featured on public radio in San Francisco, where she now lives, just north, in a small coastal town called Bolinas.

As Executive Director of a local land trust, Gail helped develop two affordable housing projects and she continues to consult to nonprofits in the areas of housing, environment and education, most recently for the Prison University Project at San Quentin Prison. More information can be found at Gailreitano.com

Sherry Stratton
After a career in technical writing, Sherry Stratton has focused on the subjects closest to her heart. Her work has been published in Bird's Thumb, Portage, Snowy Egret, A Prairie Journal, and Seeding the Snow. Sherry is copy editor for Fifth Wednesday Journal and editor of the DuPage Sierran newsletter. She and her late husband, Dick Thomas, chose a home at the edge of a forest preserve in northeastern Illinois. There, near pond and stream, she finds inspiration for her writing.

Patricia Wellingham-Jones
Patricia Wellingham-Jones has lived in an old ranch house on a creek near the top of the Sacramento Valley for 35 years. Her life revolves around the land and the seasons in this agricultural (prunes, walnuts, almonds and olives primarily) and ranching region. She is a former psychology researcher and writer/editor/publisher with articles and poetry widely published in journals, anthologies and Internet magazines. With a special interest in healing writing, she has poems recently in The Widow's Handbook (Kent State University Press). Chapbooks include Don't Turn Away: poems about breast cancer, End-Cycle: poems about caregiving, Apple Blossoms at Eye Level, Voices on the Land and Hormone Stew.

Pamela Varkony
Pamela Varkony writes what she knows: Her non-fiction topics range from politics to women's empowerment, from small town and rural Americana to historical perspectives. Pamela's view of the human condition has appeared in newspaper editorials; magazine feature stories; and on-air commentaries.

An award-winning writer, recognized by the Pennsylvania Women's Press Association for "Excellence in Journalism," and a much requested speaker, Pamela is also an advocate for women's rights and empowerment. She has worked around the world, including two fact-finding missions to Afghanistan.

Born and raised in Haycock Township, Bucks County, Pennsylvania, Pamela often weaves the lessons learned and characters encountered on those back country roads throughout her stories. Her father used to say she grew up like "a wild Indian." Pamela believes her early life filled with peace and freedom, alongside a deep love of homeland and family, is her longtime, lifetime muse.

Donna Vitucci
Donna is Development Director of Covington Ladies Home, the only free-standing personal care home exclusively for older adult women in Northern Kentucky. Her stories have appeared in dozens of print and online journals, including PANK, Fifth Wednesday Journal, Front Porch, Watershed Review, Gargoyle, Hinchas de Poesia, Contrary, Corium Magazine, Southern Women's Review, Change Seven. and most recently (this summer) The Butter. Her novel *At Bobby Trivette's Grave* will be published by Rebel E Press in 2016. Her unpublished novel *Feed Materials* was a finalist for the Bellwether Prize and is currently under agent representation. Other finished novels wait in a trunk. The pieces featured in this collection are part of her "Year of Episodic Writing." That would be this year, 2015.

Raymond M. Wong
Raymond M. Wong knows what it is to be an outsider. At age five, he left Hong Kong with his mother to come to America. In 1996, he returned to Hong Kong at age thirty-three and met a father he couldn't talk to because they spoke different languages. Words Unspoken is a series of journal entries Wong wrote to his father in 2013, an attempt to connect with a man he never really knew.

Wong is a husband and father in San Diego. He graduated with the MFA in Creative Writing from Antioch University Los Angeles. His award-winning memoir, *I'm Not Chinese:: The Journey from Resentment to Reverence*, was published by Apprentice House in 2014. His writing has appeared in *Chicken Soup for the Soul, USA Today, San Diego Union Tribune, Small Print Magazine, Segue, Marathon Literary Review*, and other publications. Visit him at www.raymondmwong.com